WORDSWORTH CLASSICS
OF WORLD LITERATURE

General Editor: Tom Griffith

THE CLOUD OF UNKNOWING

The Cloud of
Unknowing

❖

*Translated, with an Introduction,
by Mishtooni Bose*

**WORDSWORTH CLASSICS
OF WORLD LITERATURE**

For customers interested in other titles from
Wordsworth Editions visit out website at
www.wordsworth-editions.com

For our latest list and a full mail-order service contact
Bibliophile Books, 5 Thomas Road, London E14 7BN

Tel: +44 0207 515 9222   Fax: +44 0207 538 4115
e-mail: orders@bibliophilebooks.com

This edition published 2005 by Wordsworth Editions Limited
8B East Street, Ware, Hertfordshire SG12 9HJ

ISBN 1 84022 126 7

This edition © Wordsworth Editions Limited 2005
Translation and Introduction © Mishtooni Bose 2005

Wordsworth® is a registered trademark of
Wordsworth Editions Limited

1 3 5 7 9 10 8 6 4 2

Printed and bound in Great Britain by
Mackays of Chatham, Chatham, Kent

INTRODUCTION

A reluctant classic

Although the anonymous author of *The Cloud of Unknowing* and Thomas à Kempis were working in separate countries and from within different religious traditions, it is nevertheless quite possible that the present translation of *The Cloud of Unknowing* may fall into a modern reader's hands by a serendipity akin to that which brings à Kempis's words to the attention of Maggie Tulliver in George Eliot's *The Mill on the Floss* (1860):

> 'She read on and on in the old book, devouring eagerly the dialogues with the invisible Teacher, the pattern of sorrow, the source of all strength . . . She knew nothing of doctrines and systems – of mysticism or quietism: but this voice out of the far-off middle ages was the direct communication of a human soul's belief and experience, and came to Maggie as an unquestioned message.
>
> I suppose that is the reason why the small old-fashioned book, for which you need only pay sixpence at a book-stall, works miracles to this day, turning bitter waters into sweetness; while expensive sermons and treatises newly issued leave all things as they were before . . . And so it remains to all time, a lasting record of human needs and human consolations, the voice of a brother who, ages ago, felt and suffered and renounced – in the cloister, perhaps, with serge gown and tonsured head, with much chanting and long fasts, and with a fashion of speech different from ours – but under the same silent far-off heavens, and with the same passionate desires, the same strivings, the same failures, the same weariness.'

Fortunately for Maggie, the encounter with à Kempis is a fruitful one: far from being made vulnerable by her immaturity in the face of such a demanding author, she is able to use his work as a spur towards further maturation. As is well known, Eliot was concerned in this novel not merely with what would nowadays be understood as the sociology of religion, but, more specifically, with the sociology of a peculiarly etiolated form of religion, and it is despite (as much as because of) the baleful context of Maggie's spiritual quest that the words of à Kempis exert such a compelling and clarifying force in her life.

Nevertheless, as a medieval writer would have been only too aware, the encounter could have turned out very differently. Solitary, accidental and unguided, Maggie's reading of à Kempis is in many respects an all too appropriate model for many modern readers' experience of medieval spiritual texts. The immediate context in which she reads him is merely that provided by her own urgent emotional and spiritual needs. Like the modern reader who may, understandably, be more familiar with the *Cloud*'s resonant title than with its contents, Maggie is first attracted by a sense of reassuring familiarity: 'the name had come across her in her reading, and she felt the satisfaction, which every one knows, of getting some ideas to attach to a name that strays solitary in the memory.' Such is the fate of the classic, known before it is ever fully understood. Indeed, Muriel Spark's novel *The Hothouse by the East River* (1973), in whose closing paragraph a character 'trails her faithful and lithe cloud of unknowing' behind her, shows how easily the phrase can acquire a resonance independent of its original context.

This is a strange fate to have befallen *The Cloud*, whose author self-consciously presents it as a very exclusive text, suitable only for a most restricted and largely self-selecting audience. There is a sense in which modern readers, and particularly readers of the work in translation, having breached the wall that he attempts to construct in his prologue, are trespassing against his explicit intentions. Even more than is usually the case, we are reading a work which was never intended for us. An introduction which seeks to prepare the reader for this text cannot, therefore, avoid considering the implications of the spiritual 'health warning' which the *Cloud*-author sternly issues in the prologue to his work and reiterates at its conclusion.

George Eliot acknowledges but ultimately rejects the possibility that the gulf between Maggie's world and that of à Kempis is too great to be bridged. What consoles and thrills Maggie is emphatically attributed to what Eliot presents as his attractively transhistorical qualities, which seem to witness to the continuity of spiritual experience. Thus, Maggie's reading is assisted by a sense of recognition and what she feels to be the ultimately comforting notion that human nature and experience are in many ways unchanged across the centuries. What are commonly referred to as 'mystical' texts may often appear to be freighted with this particularly gratifying quality, providing an escape route whereby theology and religious experience can free themselves from the gnarled talons of history. In some ways, the *Cloud*-author may seem to invite this kind of response, refusing as he does to litter his work with references either to contemporary life or to the many theological sources upon which he has unobtrusively drawn in order to construct his introduction to contemplation. It is also typical of a work in which traditions of academic speculation are subject to chilly dismissal that the author does not merely refrain from the learned practice of documenting approved sources for his observations, but even draws attention to his policy on the matter in chapter 70: 'There was a time when men thought it an aspect of humility to say nothing original unless they confirmed it with reference to Scripture and the words of the doctors; and now this practice has degenerated into mere ingenuity and the parade of learning.'

There are other ways in which *The Cloud* may seem to shrug off its historical context. The author's strong recommendation of monosyllabic words in prayer (if words are to be used at all), together with his positive discouragement of invasive, discursive thought processes during contemplation, may be welcomed by readers with an interest in the techniques employed in Buddhism and Transcendental Meditation, who may wish to draw analogies between the practices recommended in the *Cloud* and the use of mantras. This raises the possibility that the work may acquire an aura of prescient syncretism quite alien to its author's original intention. Moreover, despite the fact that *The Cloud* is one of a small group of works known to have been produced by him, his steadfast anonymity and reluctance to reveal much about his precise clerical status, background and experience may also seem to some readers to add to this sense of timelessness. Nevertheless, further investigation of the work reveals that its author is acutely, if often very negatively, aware of the context in which he was writing and waspishly uses this awareness as a means of confronting the obstacles that surrounding cultures and the weaknesses of individuals pose to the practice of contemplation.

It is this context that is explicitly invoked in the prologue, in which the author acknowledges and regrets the fact that he cannot control the dissemination of his work. In some ways, as the author is no doubt aware, the warning issued here and repeated at the close of the work runs the risk of being counter-productive. Very few readers will be willing to identify themselves as the 'worldly wind-bags' and 'blatant braggarts' whom he identifies as the worst possible audience for his words. There is also more than a possibility that even his gentler, but no less firm insistence that the book is profoundly unsuitable for skimming may lose its force among a wide and enthusiastic readership. The prologue communicates the author's awareness of a growing constituency of readers who, while caught up in the toils of the active life, are nevertheless eager for spiritual profit and may not, therefore, be willing to discriminate properly between the comparatively accessible disciplines of meditative prayer (which he does discuss at several points in his treatise, but which do not lead to the soul's union with God) and the more specialised work of contemplation, to which comparatively few are called.

Indeed, as becomes increasingly clear throughout the book, the author places a great deal of emphasis on mastery of the art of discrimination, which assists the contemplative in critical self-scrutiny and helps him to adjudicate between profitable and unprofitable thoughts and urges. Although his book is written for one beginning the practice of contemplation, and it is later made clear that the person for whom the treatise was originally intended is only twenty-four, the author is aware that the best frame of mind with which to approach his words is one of mature self-knowledge, and he addresses himself throughout the treatise to the tensions between these facts. The prohibitions issued in the prologue are, therefore, merely the first stage of his battle against the misconceptions, the low morale, the delusions and above all the clamorous self-consciousness which may all be unavoidable ingredients of human experience, but constantly threaten to sabotage the contemplative's progress in his vocation. Although he is very far from believing that those pursuing the active life are automatically unsuitable for aspects of the contemplative life – and, in fact, lays a great deal of emphasis on the elements of interdependence between the two, a point which he elaborates upon in chapter 8 – he is concerned to point out that the most important prerequisite for a reader of his treatise is the degree of self-knowledge that makes it clear to the individual where his or her true vocation lies, and he emphatically wishes to discourage the use of his book as an accessory for those who are merely beguiled by the notion of contemplation and its mysteries.

The Cloud is, therefore, in every way a markedly reluctant classic which, far from resisting the imprint of the historical context in which it was written, was never intended to be read 'out of context'. This is, however, precisely how many readers now encounter it.

The background

The *Cloud* and its related treatises were composed during the last quarter of the fourteenth century, and the author's vigorous experiments with the stylistic resources of the English language make his work a singular and distinguished contribution to the 'renaissance' of secular and religious writing in English during this period. The *Cloud*-author is often associated with other fourteenth- and fifteenth-century English writers on the spiritual life – Richard Rolle, Walter Hilton, Margery Kempe and Julian of Norwich – and this group is often collectively referred to as the 'English mystics'. Not surprisingly, there is some evidence of contact between its members. It is known that Hilton was aware of *The Cloud* and responded to it in the second part of his treatise *The Scale of Perfection*, which was written in the 1390s. Hilton in turn featured among the canon of writers known by Margery Kempe, whose *Book* (c.1438) also contains a version of her encounter with Julian. The *Cloud*-author makes some trenchant observations about the misleading physical sensations which torment false contemplatives, including among them the feeling that a fire is burning within the breast; Rolle was the author of a treatise entitled *Incendium Amoris* (*The Fire of Love*) whose opening paragraph describes his own experience of a 'heart-warming'. Nevertheless, even leaving aside the fact that approximately a century passed between the writing of Rolle's works and the writing of Margery's *Book*, the term 'mystic', while satisfying the critic's penchant for classification, does much to obscure the important differences between these writers, and unhelpfully brackets their work away from that of their contemporaries. It also obscures the fact that this is not necessarily how they would have described themselves. Among the other treatises for which the *Cloud*-author was responsible is the translation of a Latin treatise entitled *Mystica Theologia*, itself the translation of a work, originally in Greek, by the early sixth-century writer, Pseudo-Dionysius (so-called because the identity of this writer was initially confused with that of Dionysius the Areopagite, whose conversion by St Paul is mentioned in Acts 17:34). The *Cloud*-author's choice of title, *Deonise Hid Diuinite*, indicates that his understanding of the term *mystica* was much closer to its habitual Latin sense of 'hidden' or 'secret', and the correspondingly restricted sense of the Middle English term *mystike* bears this out. The *Cloud*-author was acutely concerned with the accurate use and understanding of common terms, and it is important to take care that the label 'mystic', although now entrenched, and to that extent helpful as a form of critical shorthand, is not used to blur the differences between a range of different kinds of writing, addressing the different dimensions of individual and social religious practices.

Although the precise identity of the author remains unknown (as appears to have been his intention) there is some evidence to suggest that *The Cloud* may have been closely associated with the Carthusian order. Certainly, Carthusian houses were largely responsible for the circulation of this work (along with very many others), in the fifteenth century, and a note to a manuscript of the fifteenth-century Latin translation of the work suggests that the work's original recipient was a Carthusian. Some shadowy outlines of the relationship between the author and his original addressee are given in the work's first chapter, where the author refers to the addressee's former life in the world, from which, by grace, he was led by God 'into a more special state and form of living, to be a servant of his special servants. Here you could learn to live a more dedicated life and serve him more spiritually than you were able to do previously.' *The Cloud* may, therefore, have been intended to serve as a practical manual of spiritual instruction for a lay brother who was not familiar with Latin (as is strongly suggested in chapter 35, in which the author refers to the standard practices of *lectio*, *meditatio* and *oratio*, which are the prolegomena to contemplation, but notes that these will be better known to his pupil as 'reading, meditating and praying'). Towards the end of the book, the author reveals something more about himself, with the explicit statement that 'we have both been called by God to work at contemplation' and throughout the work looks forward to the time when his pupil will outstrip him, protesting his comparative unworthiness to teach the arts of the contemplative life and acknowledging that only the unmatched authority of experience which the novice is set to acquire will adequately answer the many questions which the book raises. In this way, therefore, as in so many others, the book urgently gestures to what lies beyond it and cannot be seen.

The work does not entirely disavow its learned context, however, and scholars have pointed out that in some respects the author is content to offer quite a derivative set of observations about human psychology in an effort to explain its possible effects on contemplation. For example, he describes a tripartite division of the human soul, largely derived from St Augustine, which was commonly used during the medieval period as a model to explain the ways in which human beings process thoughts, analyse arguments, are subject to temptations and make moral decisions. Thus, he distinguishes between the passive *mynde* (translated here as 'understanding') and the active faculties contained within it, *reson* and *wille*. He also refers to the secondary powers, *sensualite* and *imaginacioun*, the latter to be understood here in its essentially mechanical role as the power of visualisation, processing images received through the outer senses, rather than fulfilling the more elaborate function of composing fictitious narratives, as modern uses of the term often imply.

As has already been mentioned, the *Cloud*-author also drew heavily on medieval traditions of thought derived ultimately from the writings of Pseudo-Dionysius. It is clear that the *Cloud*-author wanted his readers to associate his thought with that which is expounded in the Dionysian corpus; indeed, it is for the sake of mentioning 'Seynte Denis' in chapter 70 that he breaks with his usual custom of avoiding citations. The arguments of *The Cloud*, however, are more immediately influenced by the expositions of Pseudo-Dionysius' thought in the works of Thomas Gallus, the 'Abbot of Seinte Victore' (Abbot of St Andrew's at Vercelli and a canon of the Congregation of St Victor) to whom the *Cloud*-author refers in his prologue to *Deonise Hid Divinite*. It is largely Gallus who determines the particular inflexions of Dionysian thought to be found in *The Cloud*, most notably in the *Cloud*-author's insistence, at its most explicit in chapter 6, that love is far superior to discursive thought as a means of reaching God. To a modern reader, this might seem an uncontroversial stance for the author to adopt, but there is nothing inevitable about the *Cloud*-author's having drawn such conclusions. In addition to translating *De Mystica Theologia*, he also produced an English version of the arguments in Richard of St Victor's treatise, *Benjamin Minor*, and drew on Richard's work in the concluding chapters of *The Cloud*, where he develops the analogy between Moses, Aaron and Bezaleel and three different types of contemplative experience. Richard had maintained a more positive role for reason in a process whereby the mind gradually ascended towards the contemplation of what ultimately lies beyond reason. The relative importance of reason and will was also a contested issue among twelfth- and thirteenth-century academic theologians, who were preoccupied with the question as to whether the study of theology primarily appealed to the intellect or the 'affection', that is, the individual's mental disposition or will.

As has already been noted, however, the *Cloud*-author adopts a profoundly anti-intellectual stance throughout his treatise, disparaging academic speculation, which is only presented negatively as the warped preoccupation of those in the grip of pride. Allied to this, as is made clear in chapter 56, is his brief but passionate account of the dangers of heresy, which arises, in his view, when pride leads men to 'rely excessively on their own knowledge'. Although it has not been established exactly when the *Cloud*-author was composing his treatise, it is at least possible that this reference tethers the work more securely to the 1380s, during which time certain of Wyclif's propositions were condemned as heretical and ecclesiastical opposition to his continuing influence hardened. Whether or not these references to heresy are intended as specific observations on contemporary developments, they prompt the *Cloud*-author to give only the most gross caricature of medieval intellectual culture. Nevertheless, it is not difficult to understand how this strand in his thinking melds with a more constructive insistence on the 'sharp dart of longing love' as the focus of contemplation. Thoughts may be useful and even holy in themselves, as he readily admits, but even these threaten to sabotage the work of contemplation which must, he insists, remain imageless (he uses the word *blind*), free from any extraneous intellectual or imaginative freight.

The most pervasive aspect of Dionysian influence at work in this treatise, therefore, is the *Cloud*-author's view of contemplation as an aspect of the *via negativa*, the process whereby all extraneous things, whether ideas, images or physical sensations, are rejected as the soul journeys towards contemplative union with God. In large part, the treatise deals with the many kinds of rejection that the contemplative must implement in order to clear the mind and make it a properly receptive and appropriately passive arena in which God may work. It now remains to explore the ways in which the *Cloud*-author turns this emphasis in his thought into an aspect of his style.

Negative style

Rather like the physical cloud about which the author assiduously forbids us to think in chapter 4, the treatise may give the impression of having no definite outline, particularly as the author occasionally permits himself to digress (as when considering some of the dire consequences of 'false' contemplation) and has a tendency to repeat phrases and small portions of his discussion, such as his frequent recalling of the reader's mind to the book's central depiction of contemplation: the individual aiming his 'dart' of love at the cloud of unknowing which lies between him and God. Nevertheless, in keeping with the author's acknowledgement of the ineluctable linearity of time, his treatise does progress gradually from the moment at which God calls the individual to contemplation, to a consideration of all the obstacles which lie in the contemplative's path, and then to consideration of the processes whereby sensations and thoughts are discarded and the contemplative is cured of his potentially very damaging tendency to misinterpret language used 'in the spiritual sense'.

At the beginning of the treatise, the contemplative was urged to abandon meditative processes, which can easily become confused, for contemplative ones. This occurs when he is understandably beguiled by 'meditation on God's wonderful gifts, kindness and works' or by more specific thoughts concerning 'Our Lady . . . the saints or angels in heaven . . . [or] the joys in heaven'. Such thoughts are appropriate for meditation, when the individual is positively encouraged to concentrate on particular aspects of God's glory or Christ's sacrifice, for example, but such thoughts thronging into the mind during contemplation merely distract the contemplative from his mental poise and can lead to a downward spiral, whereby he is soon reminded of his own sins and former position in the world. This discarding of images initiates a process explained throughout the treatise, whereby the individual pares away everything that hedges round the act of contemplation and separates the contemplative from his ultimate goal. The culmination of this aspect of the author's style, and of his engagement with the *via negativa* in the treatise, occurs in chapters 68 and 69, where he joyously insists on the spiritual profit to be gained from thinking of contemplation as something that takes place 'nowhere', involving the individual's 'wrestling with that imageless nothing'. From the discarding of specific images, the reader has progressed to the notion that contemplation should take place in a mental space where there is no conception even of dimensions or directions.

One of the most compelling aspects of the work's coherence is the way in which the author brings his concern with imageless contemplation to bear on the problems of addressing theological concepts 'negatively'. He is one of the pioneers of the use of the vernacular in this respect and the solutions which he finds give his work a good deal more than a merely experimental quality. He treats definition, for example, as a process of paring away everything that surrounds the essential object that he seeks to define, rather than the positive process of invoking a cluster of qualities associated with it. Although this technique was used by medieval English writers working in very different genres and styles from that of the *Cloud*-author, here it is particularly suitable as a means of expressing his general concern with the spiritual value of paring away all but the essences of things. Thus, virtue is 'nothing other than an ordered and tempered affection, plainly directed to God in himself' (chapter 12). In the following chapter, humility is 'nothing other than the true knowledge and awareness of oneself as one really is'. Prayer is 'nothing other than a devout intention, directed at God for the obtaining of blessings and the removing of evils'. The reader is constantly urged to think of sin as 'a lump', but nothing more precise than this, because it is 'nothing but itself' and the reader cannot, in any case, fully understand what it is.

It could be argued that *The Cloud* does invest in the resources of the imagination, as on the occasions on which the reader is encouraged to imagine a hypothetical situation, such as in chapter 38: 'If someone is your deadly enemy, and . . . he . . . yells out this little word "Fire!" or "Help!" . . . you rise up — yes, even though it is a winter's night! — and help him to put out his fire, or to calm down and rest in his illness.' Yet even here, it will be noted that the reader is encouraged to think in terms of a bald narrative, not a rich tableau, which would arrest the imagination and titillate the senses. The emphasis is on the argument, which urges the infinite capacity of God's mercy: the reader is not encouraged to fill out the situation with circumstantial detail, or to spend too long indulging in weighing up the conflicting feelings that might assault someone presented with the spectacle of his enemy in distress.

In keeping with its singleness of purpose and its author's diffidence about his own intellectual competence, *The Cloud* is a tactfully allusive text rather than a parade of erudition. In many ways, it glosses itself: 'difficult' or unfamiliar terms and concepts, such as that of the 'cloud of unknowing' itself, are discussed and explained within the work, and it is notable that, when defining precisely what he means by this 'cloud', the author draws upon common experience to define it afresh, rather than referring his reader to the most likely original source of the term, the phrase *nubes ignorantiae*, which had been used by Richard of St Victor. Even when dealing with this, the encapsulation of the whole work, the author prefers negative definition, telling the reader how he is *not* to think of it as a cloud in the sky. Even the closely related 'darkness of unknowing', the *caligo ignorantiae* also derived from the author's Dionysian sources, is not to be concretely visualised by the reader as the darkness which falls at night.

Maggie Tulliver, it will be remembered, profits from dialogues with an 'invisible Teacher'. The reader of *The Cloud* will notice that this, too, is a dialogic work to a certain extent, in that the author uses the notion of an inquisitive but respectful interlocutor as one means of propelling the text from topic to another, adding conversational informality and even a dramatic immediacy to its sense of purpose. Many of the chapters begin with the imagined response of the novice, whether in the form of a request for the clarification of a particular topic or something nearer to an outright challenge, such as the beginning of chapter 8, in which the interlocutor tests out a modification of the author's views concerning the thoughts which intrude upon contemplation, or the response which the author imagines him offering during the discussion of Christ's ascension. In chapter 6, the author extends the resources of the imagined dialogue by allowing his interlocutor to ask him a question which he cannot answer directly. The result of this is that the author's identity momentarily merges with that of his addressee, as he puts himself in the same position as the aspiring contemplative and models a solution to the problem: 'I wish to abandon everything that I can think about, and choose as the object of my love the thing that I can't think about, because he may be properly loved, but not properly thought about.' The imagined interlocutor has more than just questions at his disposal, however. His most plaintive and memorable intervention occurs in chapter 4, in which he berates himself for a chronic failure in time-management which, at the threshold of the contemplative life, has suddenly assumed fearful proportions.

Above all, the device of the imaginary interlocutor allows the author to insist, through continual demonstrations of such difficulties, on the practical dimensions of his discussion. Rather than compose an erudite treatise on the theory of contemplation, he uses the resources of that erudition to solve practical problems which are liable to affect any contemplative. The pedagogic imperatives of the text have further stylistic consequences, resulting in the author's anxious repetition of phrases which can be rendered as 'properly understood' or 'to put it more accurately', all bearing witness to his continual concern with accuracy of expression and interpretation. This is another kind of 'paring away', encouraging the reader to discard previous misconceptions and cherished *idées fixes*, and related to this is the author's fear lest the individual's contemplative efforts become infected by his tendency to interpret prepositions such as 'up' and 'in' too literally. This leads him to give his reader strict instructions concerning the difference between the literal and 'spiritual' senses of terms, and this, together with the technique of 'negative definition' described above, consolidates his efforts at defamiliarising the use and interpretation of apparently simple linguistic terms.

The author's attention to the realities of failure and delusion in the contemplative life occasionally call forth from him something more explicit than the dry humour with which he seeks to contain his interlocutor's putative over-enthusiasm (as when he tactfully points out that vicious self-mutilation is not a recommended practice for contemplatives). Acutely aware of the interpretative difficulties that may be brought about by ambiguities in tone or purpose, he is most anxious, for example, when he feels that his recommendation of the practice of 'flirting' with God might seem coy and immature. Elsewhere, however, he readily gives vein to broad humour (albeit arguably mingled with pathos) in his evocation of the grotesques of the contemplative life, who mistakenly substitute outward displays of giggling and gawping for the interior discipline of pure concentration.

To read The Cloud of Unknowing, therefore, is to be brought into the presence of a teacher who, however diffident, is no less exacting; and, however absorbed in his subject, is no less anxious about the potential failings of his readers. Ultimately, however, the work's modern status as a 'classic' need not be seen as an affront to its author's intentions. Works become 'classics' not because they peddle a cosily familiar view of the world but because they disrupt and reform the expectations of readers and the resources of language, and entire literary canons are composed of works that sit incongruously together, often sharing no common feature other than their refusal merely to gratify a range of established tastes. Awareness of this should make every reader of a 'classic' approach it with a constructive detachment which allows the work to speak freshly and to burst through the accretions of critical attention that it may have attracted. To approach The Cloud in such a disinterested fashion is to begin the work of 'paring away', which it enjoins on every sympathetic reader.

MISHTOONI BOSE
Christ Church, Oxford

FURTHER READING

The present text was translated from Phyllis Hodgson's edition of *The Cloud of Unknowing*, which first appeared in the Early English Text Society series, and which, together with her editions of other treatises by the *Cloud*-author, was subsequently revised and published by Analecta Cartusiana in 1982. In the later edition, Hodgson rightly insists that nothing can serve as an adequate substitute for the Middle English idioms of the original text. It is hoped, therefore, that readers of this translation will feel encouraged to explore the richness of the original: *The Cloud of Unknowing and related treatises on contemplative prayer*, ed. Phyllis Hodgson, Analecta Cartusiana 3, Salzburg and Exeter 1982.

Pseudo-Dionysius's thought may be explored further in the translation for the Classics of Western Spirituality series, *Pseudo-Dionysius: The Complete Works*, translated by Colm Luibheid with additional critical material by Paul Rorem *et al.*, Mahwah, NJ and London 1987.

Walter Hilton, *The Ladder of Perfection*, translated by Leo Sherley-Price with an introduction by Clifton Wolters (Harmondsworth 1988), offers an invaluable point of comparison with the *Cloud*-author.

Other writers mentioned in the Introduction

Thomas à Kempis (attr.), *The Imitation of Christ*, translated by B.I. Knott (London, 1996 [originally published in 1963]).

Richard Rolle, *The Fire of Love*, translated by Clifton Wolters (Harmondsworth, 1972).

Julian of Norwich, *Revelations of Divine Love* (short text and long text), translated by Elizabeth Spearing with an introduction and notes by A.C. Spearing (Harmondsworth, 1998).

The Book of Margery Kempe, translated by Barry Windeatt (Harmondsworth, 1985).

Further studies

The brief account given in this Introduction concerning the *Cloud*-author's indebtedness to Dionysian and Victorine writings draws on Alastair Minnis, 'Affection and imagination in "The Cloud of Unknowing" and Hilton's "Scale of Perfection" ', *Traditio* 39 (1983), 323–66. The Introduction also draws on the following account, which is recommended for readers wishing to gain a sense of how recent critical attention is being brought to bear on the *Cloud*-author and associated writers: Nicholas Watson, 'Middle English mystics', in *The Cambridge History of Medieval English Literature*, ed. David Wallace, Cambridge 1999, pp. 539–65.

See also

Marion Glasscoe, *English Medieval Mystics: Games of Faith*, London and New York 1993.

Simon Tugwell, *Ways of Imperfection*: *An Exploration of Christian Spirituality*, London 1984.

Christian Spirituality: High Middle Ages and Reformation, ed. Jill Raitt *et al.*, New York and London 1988.

The Study of Spirituality, ed. Cheslyn Jones *et al.*, London 1986.

TABLE OF CHAPTERS

A book of contemplation, called
THE CLOUD OF UNKNOWING
in which a soul is made one with God.

God, to whom all hearts are open, all desires speak,
and from whom nothing secret is hidden: I implore
you to cleanse the purpose of my heart with
the unutterable gift of your grace,
that I may perfectly love you
and worthily praise you.
Amen.

THE PROLOGUE

In the name of the Father and of the
Son and of the Holy Spirit.

Whoever you are who own this book (whether you own it outright, or are simply keeping it, carrying it as a messenger or borrowing it), I charge and implore you, with as much power and strength as the bond of charity may adequately permit, that (as far as you are able, purposefully and deliberately) you do not read it, copy it out, or discuss it with anyone, nor yet allow it to be read, copied out, or discussed with anyone, unless it be someone who has, to your knowledge, with proper intention and integrity of purpose, deliberately chosen to be a perfect follower of Christ, not only in the active life, but in the highest level of the contemplative life. This may be achieved through grace by a perfect soul still inhabiting this mortal body, who does what he can in order to achieve this, and, as far as you know, has already done his best for a long time in order to enable himself to live contemplatively by the virtuous means of the active life. Otherwise, it will not be at all suitable for him.

Moreover, I charge and implore you, with the authority of charity, that if any such person reads, copies out or discusses this book, or else hears it being read or spoken about or discussed, that you caution him, as I do you, to take his time thoroughly to digest it. For perhaps there is some material in it, at the beginning or in the middle, which is incomplete and not fully explained at once; and if it is not explained at that point, it is soon afterwards, or at the end. In this case, if a person saw one portion of the discussion and not the other, he might, perhaps, easily be misled. Therefore, in order to avoid misleading yourself and all others, I beg you, in charity, to do as I tell you.

I would prefer that worldly windbags, blatant braggarts, critics of themselves and others, newsmongers, gossips and tale-tellers, and all kinds of carpers should never see this book. I never intended to address such material to them. I wish, therefore, that neither they nor any of those inquisitive learned or ignorant men should meddle with it. Indeed, although they are good men, engaged in the active life, the subject-matter of this book has nothing to do with them. It may, though, have some relevance for those men outwardly leading the active life, but who are nevertheless disposed, through inward yearning after the spirit of God (whose judgements are inscrutable), and by virtue of grace, to participate in the highest level of the act of contemplation, not consistently (as is proper to authentic contemplatives) but occasionally. If such people see it, they should, by the grace of God, be greatly comforted by it.

This book is divided into seventy-five chapters. The concluding chapters teach certain signs according to which a person may authentically prove whether or not he is called by God to engage in this activity.

Dear friend in God, I implore you to pay careful attention to the progress and the nature of your vocation. Give thanks to God sincerely, so that, with the help of his grace, you may stand fast in the state, degree and form of living that you have deliberately chosen, against all the subtle assaults of your physical and spiritual enemies, and win the crown of life that lasts for ever.

Amen.

CHAPTER I

*Concerning the four degrees of Christian life, and the process
by which the person to whom this book is addressed
received his calling.*

Dear friend in God, according to my basic understanding of things,
I can distinguish four degrees and forms of Christian life, as follows:
Common, Special, Singular and Perfect. Three of these may be
started and finished in this life; and the fourth may, by grace, be
started here, but lasts for ever in the bliss of heaven. They have
been listed here in order, each one after the other – first Common,
then Special, then Singular and lastly Perfect – and so it seems to
me that, in the same order and the same course, our Lord has in his
great mercy called you and led you to him by the desire of your
heart.

First, you well know that when you were living in the Common
state of Christian life, in the company of your friends in the world,
his everlasting love (through which he made and formed you when
you were nothing, and since redeemed you with the price of his
precious blood when you were lost through Adam's sin) could not
allow you to be so far from him in form and degree of living.
Therefore, he kindled your desire, in a manner full of grace, and
fastened to it a leash of longing, and led you by this into a more
Special state and form of living, to be a servant of his special
servants. Here you could learn to live a more dedicated life and
serve him more spiritually than you were able to do previously, in
the Common state. Furthermore, it still seems that he would not
leave you so easily, because of the heartfelt love that he has always
had for you since you were born. So, what did he do? Do you not
see how easily and with what grace he has raised you to the third
degree and manner of living, which is called Singular? In this
solitary form and manner of living you may learn to lift up the foot
of your love, and walk towards the state and degree of living that is
Perfect, and the last state of all.

CHAPTER 2

A brief exhortation to humility and contemplation.

Look up now, weak wretch, and see what you are. What are you, and what have you deserved, to be called in this way by our Lord? What weary, wretched heart and slothful slumber are not roused by the draught of his love and the voice of his calling? Take care, now, wretch, with your enemy: and do not consider yourself the holier or the better because of the worthiness of this vocation and the Singular form of your life, but the more wretched and exhausted, unless you do your very best, with the help of grace and spiritual counsel, to live in accordance with that vocation. You should be more humble and loving with your spiritual spouse, since he, who is Almighty God, King of kings and Lord of lords, humbled himself so profoundly to you and graciously chose you, from amongst all his flock, to be one of his special servants, and set you in the pasture, where you may be nourished with the sweetness of his love, in anticipation of your inheritance, the kingdom of heaven.

I implore you, then, to persevere. Look ahead, now, and forget what is behind. See what you lack, and not what you possess; for that is the quickest way to attain and maintain humility. If you are to succeed in attaining the degree of Perfection, you should always be in a state of desire now. This desire should always be created in your will by the hand of Almighty God, and with your consent. I'll tell you one thing, though: he is a jealous lover and will not tolerate any competition; and he does not like working in your will unless he is alone with you. He asks for no help – only for you. He wishes only that you behold him, and leave him to do his work. Guard the windows and the door against the assaults of your enemies. If you are willing to do this, just approach him meekly in prayer, and he will soon help you.

Press on, then: let's see how you conduct yourself. He is quite ready, and waits only for you. But what must you do, and how must you make progress?

CHAPTER 3

v contemplation must be approached. Its surpassing worth.

ip your heart to God with a humble stirring of love, and
.centrate on him and not on his gifts. In order to achieve this,
.e care that you hate thinking about anything except him, so that
nothing except him may work in your understanding or in your
will. Do your best to forget all the creatures that God ever made,
and their activities, so that neither your thought nor your desire is
directed or extended towards any of them, either in general or in
particular. Leave them alone and pay them no attention.

This is the work of the soul that most pleases God. All saints and
angels take pleasure in this work, and hasten to help it with all their
power. All the devils are maddened when you do this, and try to
disrupt it in any way they can. All men living on the earth are
wonderfully helped by this work — you cannot imagine how!
Indeed, the souls in purgatory are eased of their pain by virtue of
this work. This is the most important work by which you are
cleansed and made virtuous, yet it is the easiest work of all, and the
soonest accomplished, when a soul is helped by grace in conscious
longing. Otherwise, it is hard and would be an exceptional thing
for you to achieve.

Do not give up, therefore, but work at it until you feel the
longing. For on the first occasion when you do it, you find only a
darkness and, as it were, a cloud of unknowing: you don't know
what it is, except that you feel in your will a pure concentration on
God. Whatever you do, this darkness and this cloud are between
you and your God, and get in the way of your seeing him clearly by
the light of understanding in your reason, or feeling him in the
sweetness of love in your will. Therefore, set yourself to wait in
this darkness as long as you can, always crying after him whom you
love; for if you must ever feel or see him in this life, it must always
be in this cloud and this darkness; and if you will diligently work,
as I invite you to do, I trust in his mercy that you will arrive at it.

CHAPTER 4

*Contemplation does not take a long time, and may
not be achieved by intellectual speculation,
or through the imagination.*

In order that you should not go wrong when performing this
work, and mistake its real nature, I shall tell you a little bit more
about it, as I understand it.

Contrary to what some people think, this work does not take a
long time to complete, for it is the shortest work that one can
imagine. It is neither longer not shorter than an atom – and that,
according to the definition of distinguished astronomers, is the
smallest particle of time. It is so small that, because of its minute-
ness, it is indivisible and nearly incomprehensible. This is that
'time' about which it is written: 'You shall be asked how you have
spent all the time that was given to you.' It is reasonable to request
that you should account for it, for it is neither longer nor shorter
than one impulse in your will, which is the principal active faculty
of your soul. In one hour there is the same number of impulses and
desires in your will as there are atoms. If you had been restored by
grace to the state of innocence, as man's soul was before the Fall,
then you would, with the help of that grace, be master of those
desires for ever, so that none would pass by, but all would extend
to the most desired thing of all, which is God.

For he matches the proportions of our soul by adapting his
divinity; and our soul becomes proportionate with him through the
worthiness of our creation in his image and likeness. He alone, and
nothing else, is fully sufficient, and much more besides, to fulfil the
will and desire of our soul. Moreover, by virtue of this reforming
grace, our soul is made fully adequate to grasp with love the One
who is incomprehensible to all created powers of knowing, such as
the souls of men and angels. (I am referring to their capacity to
know and not to love, and therefore I call them 'powers of
knowing' in this instance.)

All rational creatures, angels and men, individually possess one principal active faculty called a 'power of knowing', and another called a 'power of loving'. God, who made them, is always incomprehensible to the first, which is the 'power of knowing'. He is wholly comprehensible to the second, which is the power of loving in each individual, to the extent that a single loving soul could, through the power of love, grasp by itself the One who is fully sufficient – and incomparably more than this – to fill all the souls and angels that may ever exist. This is the endless, marvellous miracle of love, which shall never cease; for he shall do it forever, and never cease. Let anyone who may see by grace do so: for to feel this love is endless bliss, and the contrary is endless torment.

Therefore, if someone were reformed by grace to persevere in marshalling the stirrings of the will (since he cannot naturally exist without them), he would never be without some taste of the endless sweetness in this life, or experience the bliss of heaven without the full banquet. Therefore do not be surprised that I encourage you to contemplate. This is the work, as you shall shortly hear, at which man would have persevered if he had never sinned. It is the purpose for which he was created, and all things for him, to help him and further his purpose, and through which he shall be redeemed again. Through failure in this, a man falls deeper and deeper into sin and further and further from God. By persevering and continuously working at this activity alone, without doing anything else, a man rises higher and higher from sin, and nearer and nearer to God.

Therefore, pay good attention to the way in which you spend time, for there is nothing more precious. In a split second, heaven may be won and lost. This is a sign that time is precious: God, who creates time, never gives two moments at one, but each one after the other. He does this because he does not wish to reverse the order or the ordained course of his creation. Time is made for man and not man for time. Therefore, God, who is the ruler of nature, does not wish, when bestowing time, to anticipate the natural impulse in a man's soul, which is commensurate with each single moment. For this reason, man shall have no excuse with which to face God on Judgement Day, when he has to account for the time he has spent. It will be no good his saying: 'You give two moments simultaneously, and I have only one impulse at a time!'

But now you ruefully say: 'How shall I behave? Since what you say is true, how shall I give account of each portion of time individually – I, who never paid attention to time until now, and am now twenty-four years old? If I wished to amend this state of affairs now, you know, by virtue of what you have just written, that it is neither natural nor in keeping with the workings of common grace that I should be able to discipline or make amends for any moments other than those that lie ahead. Yes, and, what's more, I know for a fact that, because of my enormous weakness and lethargy, I shall in no way be able to discipline even one per cent of those that lie ahead of me, so I am truly confused about these things. Help me now, for the love of Jesus!'

You are right to say 'for the love of Jesus', for that is where your help lies. Love is the kind of power that enables all things to be shared. Love Jesus, therefore, and everything that he has is yours. By virtue of his divinity, he is the creator and giver of time. By virtue of his humanity, he is the true custodian of time. By virtue of his divinity and his humanity together, he is the fairest judge of the spending of time. Therefore, bind yourself to him by love and belief; and then, by virtue of that knot, you will be a co-heir with him and with all who are bound to him in such a way by love: that is to say, with our Lady, Saint Mary, who was full of grace in her use of time, with all the angels in heaven that may never waste time, and with all the saints in heaven and in earth, who, by the grace of Jesus, make disciplined use of time through the virtue of love.

Look! Here lies comfort: understand it properly and obtain some profit for yourself. But I would issue one warning: I cannot see who may truly lay claim to fellowship in this way with Jesus and with his just mother, his lofty angels and also his saints, unless it be the kind of person that does his very best, with the assistance of grace, in order to manage time. In this way, he may be seen to be making his contribution, however small, to the community, as each member does.

Therefore, pay attention to this work and to its remarkable way of acting in your soul. Properly understood, it is just a sudden and unexpected impulse, springing swiftly up to God like spark from a coal. It would be a formidable task to number the impulses that may occur in one hour in a soul that is inclined to this work, although it may be in only one of these impulses that it may have suddenly and perfectly forgotten all created things. Soon after each impulse, however, because of the corruption of the flesh, it descends again to some thought or deed that has been done, or not done. But so what? Soon afterwards, the impulse rises again as spontaneously as it did before.

This is a brief explanation of the way in which it works. It is far from being a delusion, or an imaginary vision, or an intricate idea. These are produced not by a devout, humble, unseeing impulse of love, but by a proud, speculative and ingenious intellect. If contemplation is to be properly understood, in purity of spirit, this kind of proud, speculative intellect must always be sternly trodden under foot.

Whoever hears contemplation either being read about or discussed, and thinks that it may be achieved by work in his mental faculties is dangerously deluded. He sits and searches through his mental faculties in order to work out how this can be achieved, and in this speculation makes his imagination, for example, work in an unnatural way, and invents a kind of activity which is neither physical nor spiritual. Unless God, of his great goodness, shows his mercy in a miracle and makes this person quickly abandon this work and submit himself to the advice of tried and tested contemplatives, he shall either suffer mad fits or else fall into spiritual sin and diabolical deception, through which he may easily be lost, body and soul, for ever. Therefore, for the love of God, take care in this work, and do not employ your mental faculties or your imagination in any way. I assure you, it may not be achieved by using them. Leave them and do not work with them.

Moreover, do not think that, because I call it a 'darkness' or a 'cloud', it is the kind of cloud that drifts through the sky, or the kind of darkness that falls in your house at night, when your candle is out. You may imagine this type of darkness and cloud through mental speculation, and 'see' them on the brightest summer's day; and also, conversely, you may imagine a clear shining light in the darkest winter's night. Get rid of this notion: I don't mean it in this way. When I say 'darkness', I mean a lack of knowing, just as all the things that you don't know, or else that you have forgotten, are dark to you, because you don't see them with your spiritual eye. This is why the thing that is between you and your God is not called a 'cloud of the air', but a cloud of unknowing.

CHAPTER 5

During contemplation, everything that has ever been, is now,
or ever shall be, must be hidden under the cloud of forgetting.

If you shall ever come to this cloud, and live and work in it as I
invite you to do, it is necessary that, just as this cloud of unknowing
is above you, between you and your God, you should put a
corresponding cloud of forgetting beneath you, between you and
everything that has ever been made. It may seem to you that you
are very far from God, because this cloud of unknowing is between
you and God: but if you understand it properly, you are much
further from him when you have no cloud of forgetting between
yourself and everything that has ever been made. Whenever I say
'everything that has ever been made', I mean not only the creatures
themselves, but also all their activities and states. I omit nothing,
whether physical or spiritual, nor yet any state or activity, whether
good or evil; in short, everything should be hidden under the
cloud of forgetting.

Although it may sometimes be profitable to think about certain
conditions and actions relating to some particular creatures, in this
work it is of little or no use. This is because consideration of any
creature that God ever made, or of any of their deeds, is a kind of
spiritual goal, since the eye of your soul is trained upon it and even
fixed on it, as the eye of an archer is upon his target. I tell you one
thing: everything that you think about on such occasions is above
you, between you and your God; and, to the extent that anything
is in your mind except God alone, you are so much the further
from God.

Yes, and if it isn't tactless to say so, in contemplation it is of little
or no use to think about the kindness or worthiness of God, nor
about Our Lady, nor about the saints or angels in heaven, nor yet
about the joys in heaven: that is to say, with a special attachment to
them, as if you wished, through that attachment, to nourish and
increase your sense of purpose. That is impossible with this kind of
activity, because, although it is good to think about God's kind

acts, and to love him and praise him for them, it is, nevertheless, far better to think about his pure essence, and to love him and praise him for himself.

CHAPTER 6

A short synopsis of contemplation, laid out in question-and-answer form.

Now you ask me: 'How must I think about him, and what is he?' and to this I cannot give you an answer except 'I don't know', because with that question you have brought me into the same darkness and the same cloud of unknowing that I wish you were in yourself. A man may, through grace, have comprehensive knowledge of all other creatures and their works – yes, and of the works of God himself – and may be able to think about them properly: but no one can think about God himself. Therefore I wish to abandon everything that I can think about, and choose as the object of my love the thing that I can't think about, because he may be properly loved, but not properly thought about. He may be both grasped and held by love, but neither of these things may be achieved by thought. Therefore, although it is good, sometimes, and although it is a source of enlightenment and a preliminary part of contemplation to think about the kindness and worthiness of God, in particular, nevertheless in this work it must be cast down and covered with a cloud of forgetting. You must step over it sternly but eagerly, with a devout and a pleasing stirring of love, and find the resources with which to pierce the darkness above you, and strike at that thick cloud of unknowing with a sharp dart of longing love. Do not give up, whatever happens.

CHAPTER 7

How a man must guard against all thoughts during
contemplation, and specifically against those that arise through
his own intellectual speculation and natural understanding.

If any thought rises up and always presses above you, between you
and that darkness, and questions you, saying: 'What are you
seeking, and what do you wish to obtain?' say that it is God whom
you wish to have: 'I desire him, I seek him, and nothing but him.'
If it asks you what that 'God' is, say that it is God who made you,
and redeemed you, and who has graciously called you to his love.
Say that it makes no sense, and tell it to 'Get down again!' Tread it
swiftly down with a stirring of love, even though it seems very holy
to you, and as if it would help you seek God.

For perhaps it will bring to your mind a range of attractive and
wonderful aspects of his kindness, and say that he is very sweet and
very loving, gracious and merciful. It could wish for nothing better
than that you should willingly pay attention to it, for ultimately it
will chatter more and more in this manner until it brings you lower
down, to the conception of his Passion. There, it will let you see
the wonderful kindness of God, and it could ask for no better thing
than if you were to pay it attention, for, soon after, it will let you
see your old, wretched way of life; and, perhaps, when you are
seeing this and thinking about it, it will bring into your mind some
place where you lived before now. Ultimately, before you know
it, your concentration will be shattered and you won't know what
has happened to it. The cause of this dissipation is that, at first, you
willingly paid attention to that thought, answered it, accepted it,
and let it work unhindered.

Nevertheless, what it said was both good and holy; yes, and so
holy that the man or woman that thinks to come to contemplation
without this kind of sweet meditation, in advance, on his or her
own wretchedness, the Passion, the kindness and the great goodness
and worthiness of God, will surely go wrong and fail to achieve his
or her aim. Nevertheless, a person who has spent a long time in

these meditations must always abandon them, and put them aside, and keep them far down under the cloud of forgetting, if he is ever to pierce the cloud of unknowing between him and God.

Therefore, whenever you decide to engage in this work, and feel by grace that you have been called by God, lift up your heart to God with a humble impulse of love, and concentrate on God who made you, and redeemed you, and who has graciously called you to this work; and do not entertain any other thought about God. Moreover, do not do all these things, but only those that suit you, because a pure concentration on God, without consideration of anything else, will suffice.

If you would like to have this kind of concentration encapsulated in a single word, so that you should have a better grasp of it, use only a monosyllabic word. This is better than a polysyllabic word, because the shorter it is, the better it suits the work of the spirit. The word 'God' or 'Love' is like this. Choose whichever you prefer, or another one, as it suits you: whichever monosyllabic word you like best. Impress this word on your heart, so that it never leaves it, whatever happens.

This word shall be your shield and your spear, whether you ride in peace or war. You must beat at the cloud and the darkness above you with this word. With this word you must strike down all kinds of thoughts under the cloud of forgetting, to the extent that if any thought presses upon you, asking you what you desire, answer it with no words except this one. If it offers, from the standpoint of its great learning, to expound that word to you and to tell you its aspects, tell it that you want the word whole, not analysed to bits. If you hold fast to this aim, such a thought will surely not trouble you for long – and why? Because you would not let it feed on the kind of sweet meditations which I described previously.

CHAPTER 8

A clear account of certain doubts that may arise during this
work, laid out in question-and-answer form. How to destroy
one's own intellectual speculation and natural understanding,
and to distinguish the levels of active and contemplative life.

But now you ask me, 'What is disturbing me in this work? Is it
good or evil? If it is something evil', you say, 'then I am amazed
that it should increase someone's devotion so much, for sometimes
it seems to me that it is a comfort to listen to what it says.
Sometimes, I find, it makes me weep vehemently for pity over the
Passion of Christ, sometimes for my wretchedness, and for many
other reasons that seem very holy to me, and do me much good.
Therefore, it seems to me that it cannot be evil. If it is good, and
does me so much good with its sweet suggestions, then I am
amazed that you should command me to lay it to one side, and to
put it so far away under the cloud of forgetting.'

I think that this is a very good question, and therefore I will
answer it as well as my feeble understanding will permit. First, when
you ask me what it is that intrudes so harshly on you, offering to help
you in this work, I answer that it is a sharp and clear perception from
your natural understanding, engraved in your reason within your
soul. When you ask me whether it is good or evil, I reply that it must
naturally always be good, because reason is a spark of the image of
God. Its use, however, may be both good and evil. It is good when
it is alerted through grace to see your wretchedness, the Passion, the
kindness and the wonderful works of God in physical and spiritual
creations; and then it is no wonder that it increases your devotion so
much, as you say. But reason is evil when it is swollen with pride,
and with the arrogant speculation that comes from too much
learning and academic scholarship, as in the case of clerks. It makes
them strain at the leash not to be considered humble scholars and
masters of divinity or of devotion, but proud scholars of the devil,
and masters of vanity and falsehood. In other men or women,
whatever their status, whether religious or lay, the employment of

this natural intelligence is evil when it is swollen with pride and with the inquisitive strategies associated with worldly objects and material preoccupations, in the coveting of worldly reputations and the obtaining of riches, vacuous pleasures and flattery.

When you ask me why you must put it down under the cloud of forgetting – since it is naturally good, and, when properly used, does you a great deal of good and increases your devotion so much – I respond that you must understand that there are two ways of leading the Christian life. One is the active and the other is the contemplative life. The active is lower, and the contemplative higher. The active life has two degrees, one higher and one lower; the contemplative life also has two degrees, one lower and one higher. These lives are so joined together that, although they are very different in some respects, nevertheless neither of them may be fully experienced without some aspects of the other. For this reason, the higher part of the active life is the lower part of the contemplative life, so that a man may not be fully active unless he is partly contemplative, nor yet fully contemplative, in this life, unless he is in part active. The nature of the active life is such that it is both begun and completed in this life. The same is not true of the contemplative life: that is started in this life, and lasts forever, because the part that Mary chose shall never be taken away from her. The active life is preoccupied with many things, but the contemplative rests peacefully with a single object.

The lower part of the active life consists in good, honest social works of mercy and charity. The higher part of the active life, and the lower of the contemplative life, lies in good spiritual meditations and diligent consideration of a man's own wretchedness, with sorrow and contrition; compassionate consideration of the Passion of Christ and of his servants; and grateful consideration of the wonderful gifts, kindness and works of God in all his physical and spiritual creations. The higher part of contemplation, as experienced in this life, is, however, wholly suspended in the darkness and the cloud of unknowing, with a loving impulse and an imageless conception of the pure essence of God himself.

In the lower part of the active life, a man is outside himself and beneath himself. In the higher part of the active life and the lower part of the contemplative life, a man is within himself and equal to himself. But in the higher part of the contemplative life, a man is above himself and under his God. He is above himself, because he is determined to achieve that position by grace, though he may not arrive at it through nature alone – that is to say to be knit to God in spirit, and in unity of love and will.

Just as it is inconceivable to a human being that a man should arrive at the higher part of the active life unless he temporarily ceases the activity of the lower part, so a man may not arrive at the higher part of the contemplative life unless he temporarily ceases the lower activity. Just as it is unlawful, and would prevent a man that sat at meditation, to consider his outward, bodily works, which he had done, or else had to do, even if they were very holy works in themselves – then just as certainly is it improper, and would just as much hinder a man that had to work in this darkness and in this cloud of unknowing with an emotional stirring of love for God in himself, if he allowed any thought or any meditation on God's wonderful gifts, kindness and works in any of his creatures, whether physical or spiritual, to creep up on him and insert themselves between him and his God, no matter how holy, pleasing and comfortable they were.

It is for this reason that I command you to repress this kind of sharp, subtle thought, and to cover it with a thick cloud of forgetting, no matter how holy it is, nor how much it promises to help you in your task. For love may reach up to God in this life, but knowing may not; and as long as the soul inhabits this mortal body, the acuteness of our understanding of all spiritual matters, and particularly of God, is contaminated with some kind of self-deception, which contaminates our work and, unless that was of a most exceptional quality, would lead us into a great deal of error.

CHAPTER 9

*During contemplation, consideration of the holiest creature
that God ever made hinders more than it helps.*

Therefore, the sharp impulse from your understanding, that will
always intrude upon you when you address yourself to this
imageless work, must always be trodden down. Unless you repress
it, it will wear you down, to the extent that when you think that
you are properly waiting in this darkness, and that nothing is in
your mind except God alone, if you look more closely, you shall
find your mind occupied not with this darkness but with a keen
consideration of something beneath God. If this is the case, that
object is definitely above you, temporarily between you and God.
Therefore, be determined to repress such preoccupations, no
matter how pious or pleasant they are.

I tell you one thing: it is of more value to the health of your soul,
more worthy in itself and more pleasing to God and to all the saints
and angels in heaven – yes, and more helpful for all your friends,
whether social or spiritual, alive or dead – to aim this kind of
imageless, intimate impulse of love for God alone at this cloud of
unknowing. It is better for you to have it and to feel it spiritually,
in your will, than it is to have the eye of your soul gazing in
contemplation or consideration of all the angels of saints in heaven,
or in hearing all the cheerful sounds and melodious music that they
share in bliss.

Do not be surprised at this, for if you could see it just once as
clearly as grace will permit you to feel your way towards it in this
life, you would agree with what I say. Be sure, though, that no one
shall ever have that clarity of perception in this life – one may have
an intimation of it through grace, when God permits. Therefore,
lift up your love to that cloud. To put it more accurately, let God
draw your love up to that cloud, and try, through the help of his
grace, to forget all other things.

Since the pure consideration of anything beneath God, oppressing
your will and your consciousness, puts you further from God than

you would be if it did not exist, and hinders you, and makes you to that extent less able to experience the fruit of his love, how can you not realise that conscious, voluntary thought about anything suggested to you will hinder you in your purpose? Since thinking about any particular saint or any pure spiritual object will hinder you so much, how can you not realise that the thought of anyone in this wretched life, or of any kind of concrete or abstract object will impede you in this activity?

Although it is a hindrance to this kind of work, I am not saying that this kind of raw, sudden thought about any good, pure, spiritual object beneath God, oppressing your will or your consciousness, or else willingly entertained by you on purpose, in order to increase your devotion, is therefore evil. No, God forbid that you should think this. But although it is good and holy, it hinders more than it helps while you are engaged in contemplation. The one who perfectly seeks God will surely not rest content with thoughts about any angel or saint in heaven.

CHAPTER 10

How to know when a thought is not sinful; if it is sinful,
when it is a mortal and when a venial sin.

Nevertheless, thinking about a person, or about any concrete or abstract object, is not to be viewed leniently. Although it is not a sin with which you may be charged (because it is the torment of original sin oppressing your strength, and you are cleansed of this in baptism), unless a raw, sudden thought about any of these things, intruding on your will and your consciousness, is not quickly repressed, then your natural disposition will be influenced by it towards affection, if it is something that pleases you or has pleased you before, or else with displeasure, if it is something that you think irks you or has irritated you previously. In men and women living in the world, who were in a state of mortal sin beforehand, this kind of attachment is a mortal sin; nevertheless, such predilection or displeasure, overwhelming the natural disposition, is only a venial sin in you and in all others who have forsaken the world with a true sense of purpose.* This is because, witnessed and advised by a judicious spiritual adviser, you anchored your purpose in God at the beginning of the current phase of your life. But if this predilection or displeasure, affecting your natural inclination and that of others, is allowed to remain there for so long without rebuke that it is ultimately rooted in your will with your full consent, then it is a mortal sin.

This happens when you, or any of the other people whom I mentioned earlier, voluntarily entertain the thought of a living person, or any other concrete or abstract object, to the extent that

---

* *Venial sin* is a grave offence against God's purpose, but does not wholly deprive the soul of grace. *Mortal sin*, on the other hand, involves a deliberate turning away from God's purpose. It is committed when an individual voluntarily accedes to the sinful act, and thereby incurs the risk of eternal damnation.

if it is something that irritates you, or has done so before, an angry passion and an appetite for revenge, called wrath, rises up in you; or else a cruel disdain, and a kind of loathing of a person, with harsh and reproachful thoughts, which is called envy; or else a weariness and a disinclination for any decent occupation, whether physical or spiritual, which is called sloth. If it is something that pleases you, or has done so before, an immoderate delight in thinking about it rises up in you, so that you wallow in that thought, and ultimately fasten your heart and your will on it, and gorge your natural inclination on it, so that you feel that you covet no other kind of wealth than to live for ever in this peace and rest with you favourite thought. If the thought that you entertain, or else accept when it is suggested to you and rest yourself in complacently, concerns worth of nature or knowledge, grace or status, favour or beauty, then it is pride. If it concerns any kind of worldly good, riches or possessions, or anything that a man may possess or be lord of, then it is avarice. If it is gourmet food and drink, or any kind of pleasure for the taste buds, then it is gluttony. If it is lust or sensual pleasure, or any kind of physical stimulation, blandishment or flattery of anyone, or of yourself, then it is lechery.

CHAPTER II

One must judge each thought and each desire, and always
avoid carelessness in committing venial sin.

I do not say this because I think that you, or anyone else of the kind
that I mentioned earlier, are guilty and burdened with any such
sins, but because I want you to judge each thought and each
impulse, and because I want you to work diligently to destroy the
first suggestion of anything that may cause you to sin. I'll tell you
one thing: whoever does not govern his first thought, or under-
estimates its power – yes, even if it is no sin for him – will not avoid
carelessness in committing venial sin. No man can entirely avoid
venial sin in this mortal life, but carelessness in committing venial
sin should always be avoided by all true disciples of perfection. If
they do not do this, I would not be surprised if they should soon
commit mortal sins.

CHAPTER 12

*Sin is destroyed and virtues are engendered
through the power of contemplation.*

Therefore, if you wish to stand firm and not fall, never abandon
your intention, but keep on beating forever with a sharp dart of
longing love at this cloud of unknowing that is between you and
God. Detest thoughts of anything beneath God, and do not give
up, whatever happens. For this alone is the work that destroys the
ground and the root of sin. No matter how much you fast, stay
awake in vigils, rise early, lie down uncomfortably, wear an
irritating hairshirt – yes, even if it were permitted (which it isn't)
for you to put out your eyes, cut out your tongue, block up your
ears and your nose; even if you sheared off your private parts and
inflicted every torment on your body that you could dream up – all
this would be of absolutely no use to you: the impulse and
gravitation towards sin would still be in you.

Yes, and what's more, no matter how much you weep for
sorrow over your sins, or over the Passion of Christ; no matter
how much you think about the joys of heaven – what do you
achieve? Certainly it will do you a great deal of good, be a great
help to you and be of benefit and obtain a great deal of grace for
you. But in comparison with this imageless impulse of love, it will
achieve only a small amount. This, by itself, is Mary's 'best part'.
Without it, the other activities are of little or no benefit. It not only
destroys the foundation and the root of sin, as far as that may be
achieved in this life, but also obtains great virtues. For, if it is
properly understood, all virtues shall be intricately and perfectly
understood and grasped by it, without any contamination from
self-conscious effort. However many virtues a man has without it,
they are all contaminated with some fallible effort, which makes
them imperfect.

Virtue is nothing other than an ordered and tempered affection,
plainly directed to God in himself. For this reason, he in himself is
the pure cause of all virtues, to the extent that if any man is stirred

towards any particular virtue for any other reason – yes, even though God were the chief cause of it – then that virtue will still be imperfect. This may, for example, be seen in the case of a couple of virtues, namely humility and charity, for whoever obtains these two needs no more. Through these, he has them all.

CHAPTER 13

The nature of humility: when it is perfect and when imperfect.

Let's first consider the virtue of humility. It is imperfect when it is caused by any other thing besides God, even if he is its chief cause, and perfect when it is caused by God alone. First, you need to understand what humility is in itself, and this matter shall be clearly explained; afterwards, we may more accurately and truly understand what causes it.

Humility in itself is nothing other than the true knowledge and awareness of oneself as one really is. Anyone who could truly see and feel what he is would be properly humble. This humility has two causes: one is the filth, the wretchedness and the frailty into which man has fallen through sin, and which he must always feel to some degree while alive, however holy he is. Another is the superabundant love and the worthiness of God in himself: in contemplating this, all nature quakes, all academics are fools and all saints and angels are blind, to the extent that if God, through his divine wisdom, did not moderate their levels of perception according to the abilities they acquire through nature and grace, I dread to say what would happen to them.

The second cause is perfect, and shall therefore last eternally. The first cause is imperfect, and for this reason, not only is it transitory, but very often, because the abundance of grace increases its desire, as often and as long as God brings this about, a soul in this mortal body shall suddenly and perfectly have lost and forgotten all consciousness of its existence, not fretting as to whether it has been holy or wretched. Whether someone suitably disposed experiences this often or only occasionally, however, it only lasts a short while. During this time, he is perfectly humbled, because he knows and feels no cause but the chief one. When he knows and feels another cause to be mixed up with it, it is still imperfect humility, even if God is its chief cause. Nevertheless, this is still good and must always be experienced: and God forbid that you should misunderstand me on this point.

CHAPTER 14

Without the prerequisite of imperfect humility, it is impossible
for a sinner to attain perfect humility in this life.

Although I call this imperfect humility, nevertheless I would rather
have accurate knowledge and experience of myself as I am, and I
believe that this would sooner obtain for me the perfect virtue of
humility by itself, than it would if all the saints and angels in
heaven, and all the men and women in the Church, in all degrees,
whether religious or secular, were together to dedicate themselves
to doing nothing else but praying to God for my sake, to obtain
perfect humility for me. Indeed, it is impossible for a sinner to
obtain the perfect virtue of humility, or to keep it when it has been
obtained, without this.

Therefore, work hard and sweat at it as much as you can, in order
to obtain a true knowledge and awareness of your true nature.
Soon after this, I believe, you will have a true knowledge and sense
of God's true nature; not as he is in himself, for no man may have
that except him; nor yet as you shall do in bliss, both body and soul
together; but as it is possible to know and feel him (and as he allows
himself to be known and felt) by a humble soul inhabiting this
mortal body.

Because I distinguish two causes of humility, one perfect and
another imperfect, do not think that I therefore wish that you
should abandon striving for the imperfect humility and wholly
dedicate yourself to achieving the perfect kind. No, truly, I think
that you would never achieve it in this way. I put it this way
because I want to let you see the worthiness of this spiritual
exercise above all others, whether physical or spiritual, that man
may perform by grace – how the thrust of intimate love, aimed in
purity of spirit at this dark cloud of unknowing between you and
God, subtly and absolutely contains in itself the perfect virtue of
humility, without any specific or clear perception of anything
beneath God; and because I want you to know what perfect
humility is, and to set it as a goal for your heart's desire, and to do

this for your sake and mine; and because I wish that you should increase in humility through this knowledge.

I think that ignorance is often the cause of much pride. Perhaps, if you did not know what perfect humility was, when you had a little knowledge and an awareness of what I call imperfect humility, you would think that you had almost obtained perfect humility; and in this way you would deceive yourself, and think that you were completely humble, when you were swathed in foul, stinking pride. Therefore, dedicate yourself to working at perfect humility, because its nature is such that whoever has it shall not sin while he has it, nor yet much after that.

CHAPTER 15

*A brief confutation of those who mistakenly
maintain that consciousness of one's
own wretchedness is the most perfect
cause of humility.*

Trust steadfastly that this kind of perfect humility does exist, and
may be achieved through grace in this life. I say this in order to
confute the error of those who say that the awareness of our
wretchedness and previously committed sin is the most perfect
cause of humility. I grant that, for those who, like me, have been
habitual sinners, the most necessary and successful cause is to be
humbled through the consciousness of one's wretchedness and
previously committed sins, until the great rust of sin is for the most
part rubbed away, with one's conscience and spiritual director as
witnesses of this process.

But for others, who are innocent, and have never intentionally
and deliberately committed mortal sin, except through frailty and
ignorance, and who dedicate themselves to the contemplative
life – and for us both, if our directors and our consciences witness
our lawful amendment in contrition, confession and satisfaction
according to the practices of Holy Church, and if we feel ourselves
impelled and called by grace to be contemplatives – there is
another cause through which to be humbled, as far above this first
cause as is the life of our Lady Saint Mary above the life of the most
sinful penitent in Holy Church; or the life of Christ above the life
of any other man in this life; or else the life of an angel in heaven,
who never experiences frailty of spirit, above the life of the most
feeble man in this world.

If there was no perfect cause through which to be humbled
except the experience of wretchedness, then I would like those
who think this to explain to me how those who never experience
wretchedness or the impulse to sin, such as our Lord Jesus Christ,
our Lady Saint Mary and all the saints and angels in heaven, achieve
humility. Our Lord Jesus Christ called us himself in the Gospel to

this state of perfection,* among others, when he commands that we should be perfect by grace, just as he is by nature.

* 'Our Lord Jesus Christ . . . state of perfection': Matthew 5:48.

CHAPTER 16

A sinner who has truly converted and has been called to
contemplation attains perfection sooner by this than by
any other work. Through contemplation he may more
rapidly obtain God's forgiveness for his sins.

Let no one think it presumptuous that, after he has lawfully made
amends, and has felt himself compelled towards the life that is
called contemplative, with the agreement of his director and his
conscience, the most wretched sinner in this life dare take it upon
himself to offer a humble impulse of love to his God, striking in
secret at the cloud of unknowing between him and God. When
our Lord said to Mary Magdalene (who personifies all sinners
called to the contemplative life) 'Your sins are forgiven you',* he
did so not because of her great sorrow, or because of her awareness
of her sins, nor yet because of the humility that she experienced
when contemplating her wretchedness. Why, then? Surely because
she felt a great love. Look! Here people may see what the thrust of
intimate love may obtain from our Lord, above all other activities
that anyone could imagine.

Yet I grant that she experienced much sorrow, and wept very
bitterly for her sins, and was sincerely humbled through consciousness of her wretchedness. So should we, who have been wretches
and habitual sinners all our life: we should experience hideous and
remarkable sorrow for our sins and be very humbled by the
awareness of our wretchedness.

But how can we do this? Just as Mary did. She could not abandon
the feeling of the deep, intimate sorrow for her sins, because all her
life she had them with her, wherever she went, as if they had been
bound up together in a bundle and laid intimately in the chamber
of her heart, never to be forgotten. Nevertheless, Scripture declares
that she experienced a yet more profound sorrow, a more bitter

---

* 'When our Lord said to Mary Magdalene . . . forgiven you': Luke 7:47–8.

yearning, and that she sighed all the more deeply and languished all the more − even to death, in fact − for lack of love, rather than because of the awareness of her sins. She did this even though she already felt a great deal of love. So, do not be surprised at it, for the condition of a true lover is that the more he loves, the more he desires to love.

Still, she acknowledged and felt, in sober truth, that she was a wretch more foul than any other, and that her sins had created a division between her and God, whom she loved so much; and also that they were to a large extent the cause of her languishing for lack of love. But what of this? Did she therefore descend from the height of desire into the depths of her sinful life, and search in the foul, stinking bog and dunghill of her sins, raking through them one by one, with all their particular circumstances, and sorrow and weep over each one individually? No, she certainly did not. Why? Because, through his grace, God let her realise that she would never achieve this, since she would sooner stimulate her ability to sin again through such behaviour than obtain forgiveness for all her sins.

Therefore, she suspended her love and her longing desire in this cloud of unknowing, and learned to love a thing which she could not see clearly in this life by the light of understanding in her reason, not yet truly feel in the sweetness of love in her will, to the extent that she often ceased to care about whether or not she had ever been a sinner. I think that, very often, she was so deeply immersed in the love of his divinity that she paid very little attention to the beauty of his precious and blessed body, in which form he sat very lovingly, speaking and preaching before her − nor yet to anything else, whether physical or spiritual. The Gospel tells us that this is true.

CHAPTER 17

A proper contemplative does not wish to have any dealings
with the active life. He neither cares about anything that is
said or done concerning him, nor bothers to answer his critics.

In Saint Luke's gospel it is written that when our Lord was in the
house of Martha her sister, Mary sat at his feet all the time that
Martha busied herself with the arrangements for the meal.* En-
grossed in his words, she paid no attention to her sister's activity,
although it was very good and holy, for it is the first part of the
active life – nor yet to the beauty of his blessed body, nor to the
sweet voice and words of his human form, although this is better
and holier, for it is the second part of the active life and the first part
of the contemplative life. She concentrated on the highest source
of the wisdom of his divinity, which was contained in the cryptic
words of his humanity. She concentrated on this with all the love
of her heart. She did not wish to remove herself from this on
account of anything that she saw or heard around her, but sat very
still, with much sweet, intimate and yearning love aimed at that
high cloud of unknowing between her and God.

I'll tell you one thing: there was never yet, nor ever shall be, a
pure creature in this life that was ravished to such a height in the
contemplation and love of the Godhead that there is not always a
high and remarkable cloud of unknowing between him and God.
It was in this cloud that Mary was occupied with many movements
of intimate love – and why? Because it was the best and the holiest
part of contemplation that may be experienced in this life. She
would not remove herself from this for anything, so that when her
sister Martha complained to our Lord about her, and asked him to
order her sister to get up and help her, and not let her work and
labour by herself, she sat very still and did not answer with a single

---

* 'In Saint Luke's gospel . . . ' Luke 10:38–42. Note that Mary of Bethany,
sister of Martha and Lazarus, was often conflated with Mary Magdalene (see
above, chapter 16) in medieval exegesis.

word, nor showed so much as an angry expression at her sister, whatever her complaints – and no wonder. For she had another task to perform, which Martha did not know about, and therefore she had no time to listen to her, or respond to her complaint.

Look at this: all the words and the behaviour that our Lord and these two sisters displayed have been set down as an example for all the actives and contemplatives that have lived since that time in Holy Church, and shall do until Judgement Day. All contemplatives are represented by Mary, and actives by Martha, because they must conform their respective ways of life accordingly.

CHAPTER 18

How actives still complain about contemplatives nowadays,
as Martha did about Mary: and that ignorance is
the cause of such complaining.

Just as Martha complained then about Mary her sister, so all
actives still complain about contemplatives. Let us suppose there
is a man or a woman in any community in this world – whatever
community it be, whether religious or lay – who feels impelled
through grace and by spiritual advice to abandon all external
preoccupations, and to dedicate themselves wholly to living the
contemplative life in accordance with their understanding and
their conscience, with the agreement of their director. Just as
readily, their own brothers and sisters, and all their friends beyond
that, together with many others who do not understand their
compulsion, nor the way of living to which they have dedicated
themselves, will rise against them in a spirit of deep dissatisfaction,
and say brusquely to them that what they are doing counts for
nothing. Just as readily, these people will rake up many false
stories, and many truthful ones too, concerning the fall of men
and women who previously dedicated themselves to such a life,
and will never relate the encouraging stories about the ones who
persevere.

I accept that many of those who have forsaken the world in this
way do fall, and have fallen. Because they would not regulate their
lives by true spiritual counsel, instead of becoming God's servants
and his contemplatives, they have become the devil's servants and
his contemplatives, and have turned either into hypocrites or
heretics, or fall into mania and many other dire straits, to the
disgrace of Holy Church. I will leave off speaking about them at
this point, because it interrupts the course of our subject. Later on,
however, if the need arises and God permits it, I will explain
something of their plight and the reasons behind their fall. I will
not say more about them at this point. Let's continue with our
subject.

CHAPTER 19

The author teaches that all contemplatives should excuse
all actives their plaintive words and unhelpful deeds.

Some might think that I pay scant respect to Martha, that special
saint, because I compare her plaintive remarks about her sister with
the words of these worldly people, or theirs with hers. Truly, I
don't mean to discredit either her or them. God forbid that I should
say anything in this work that might be taken as a rebuke to any of
God's servants, in any degree, and particularly to his special saint. It
seems to me that, if one takes note of the occasion and the manner
in which she expressed herself, she should be fully excused her
complaint. She was ignorant of the cause of what had annoyed her;
and it is no wonder that she did not know on that occasion what
Mary was doing, for I think that before that occasion she had heard
little about such perfection. Moreover, she spoke courteously and
concisely, and so should always be excused.

Thus, I think that, although they speak brusquely, these worldly
people engaged in the active life should also be fully excused the
plaintive words described above, and their ignorance should be taken
into consideration. Just as Martha knew very little about what her sister
Mary was doing when she complained about her to our Lord, so in the
same way these people nowadays know very little, or else nothing,
about what these young disciples of God are aiming at when they set
themselves apart from the bustle of this world and withdraw to be
God's special servants in holiness and righteousness of spirit. If they
understood it, I dare say that they would neither act nor speak in this
way. It seems to me, therefore, that they should always be excused,
because they know no better way of life than that which they follow
themselves. Also, when I consider the innumerable mistakes which I
have made both in my words and actions because of my incomplete
knowledge, I think that if I wish to be excused by God for my ignorant
failings, then I should always excuse other people's ignorant words and
deeds, charitably and compassionately. Otherwise, I am not behaving
towards others as I would have them behave towards me.

CHAPTER 20

How Almighty God will answer sufficiently on behalf of all
those that do not wish to abandon the task of loving him.

I think, therefore, that those who dedicate themselves to being contemplatives should not only excuse active men their words of complaint, but also should be so spiritually occupied that they pay little or no attention to what people do or say around them. This is the way Mary, our supreme example, behaved when Martha her sister complained to our Lord. If we truly behave in this way, our Lord will act for us now as he did then for Mary.

He acted in this manner: although our precious Lord, Jesus Christ, from whom no secret thing is hidden, was required by Martha to act as referee, to command Mary to rise and help her to serve him, because he perceived that Mary was fervently occupied in her spirit with the love of his Godhead, he courteously and rationally answered on her behalf, so that she would not be distracted from loving him in order to excuse herself. How did he answer? Certainly not as a mere adjudicator, as Martha called on him to act, but as a lawyer might legally defend someone who loved him, and said 'Martha, Martha!' He called her twice, in haste, because he wanted her to hear him and to pay attention to his words. 'You are very busy', he said, 'and preoccupied with many things.' Actives must always be busy and preoccupied with many different matters: firstly those which affect their own lives, and secondly, deeds of mercy performed for their fellow-Christians, as charity requires. He said this to Martha because he wanted to let her know that her occupation was good and profitable for the health of her soul. But in order that she should not think that it was the loftiest task that a person might perform, he added to this and said 'but one thing is necessary'.

What is that 'one thing'? It is that God be loved and praised by himself, above all other activities, whether physical or spiritual, that anyone might perform. Martha could not think that she could love God and praise him above all other activities, physical or spiritual, and also be preoccupied about the necessities of this life. Therefore, in order to relieve her from the suspicion that she could not serve God perfectly through a combination of physical and spiritual activity (for she could do so imperfectly, but not perfectly), he added something further, and said that Mary had chosen the best part, which should never be taken from her. For the perfect stirring of love that commences here is equal in substance with that which shall last eternally in the bliss of heaven; for it is all one.

CHAPTER 21

The true interpretation of this declaration from the Gospel:
'Mary has chosen the best part.'

What does 'Mary has chosen the best' mean? Wherever 'the best' is mentioned, it raises these two other possibilities, a 'good' and a 'better', in order that it should be the best, and the third in the sequence. But what are these three good things, of which Mary chose the best? They are not three lives, because Holy Church only recognises two, the active life and contemplative life, and these two lives are allegorically depicted in the Gospel story of these two sisters, Martha and Mary, with Martha as the active life and Mary the contemplative. No man may be saved except through one of these two lives; and where there are no more than two, no man may choose the 'best'.

Although there are only two lives, however, within these two lives there are three parts, each one better than the other. These three categories have individually been laid out and described above. As was said before, the first part consists in good and honest social works of mercy and charity; and this is the first degree of the active life, as I said before. The second part of these two lives lies in good spiritual meditations concerning one's own wretchedness, the Passion of Christ, and the joys of heaven. The first part is good, and this part is better, for this is the second degree of active life and the first of the contemplative life. In this category, the contemplative and active lives are joined together in a spiritual relationship and turned into 'sisters', following the example of Martha and Mary. An active may ascend this high towards contemplation, and no higher, unless very occasionally and through a special grace. A contemplative may descend this far down towards the active life, and no further, unless very occasionally, and in great necessity.

The third part of these two lives is suspended in the dark cloud of unknowing, with many a secret motion of love towards God himself. The first part is good, the second is better, but the third is the best of all. This is Mary's 'best part', and therefore it should plainly be understood that our Lord did not say 'Mary has chosen the best life', for there are no more than two lives, and no man may choose the best of two. Of these two lives, 'Mary', he said, 'has chosen the best part, which shall never be taken from her'. Although the first and the second part are both good and holy, nevertheless they end when this life ceases. In the next life, there will be no need to perform works of mercy, or to weep for our wretchedness, or for the Passion of Christ. For then, as now, none shall hunger or thirst, nor die for cold, nor be ill, nor homeless, nor in prison, nor yet require burial, for then none shall die. But let anyone who is called by grace choose the third part, with Mary: or, to speak more accurately, let whoever is chosen by God be cheerfully inclined to perform that task. That shall never be taken away: if it commences here, it shall last forever.

Therefore, let the voice of our Lord cry out to these actives, as if he spoke now to them on our behalf, as he did then to Martha on Mary's behalf: 'Martha, Martha!' 'Actives, actives! Keep yourselves busy in both parts, now in one and now in the other; and, if you have the inclination and feel disposed towards it, do both, using the resources of your physical life. Don't interfere with contemplatives. You don't know what their concerns are. Let them sit at their rest and their recreation, with the third and best part of Mary.'

CHAPTER 22

The remarkable love that Christ had for Mary, who
personifies all sinners who have truly converted
and been called to the grace of contemplation.

There was tender love between our Lord and Mary. She had much love for him; he had much more for her. If anyone could see the way they behaved towards each other (not as a scandal-monger might, but as the Gospel story, which cannot be inaccurate, narrates) they would find that she was so fervently dedicated to loving him that nothing beneath him could comfort her, nor yet distract her heart from him. This is that same Mary, who, when she sought him tearfully at the sepulchre, would not be comforted by the angels. When they spoke so sweetly and lovingly to her, and said 'Do not cry, Mary; for our Lord, whom you seek, has risen, and you shall have him, and see him alive and fair amongst his disciples in Galilee, as he promised',* she would not leave on their account, because she thought that whoever really sought the King of angels would not wish to leave on account of mere angels.

There is more to this. Whoever reads the Gospel story properly shall find many wonderful aspects of perfect love written about in relation to her, as an example to us, and in ways that are most relevant to the present treatise, as has been mentioned previously. They were truthful: let whoever may profit by them do so. If anyone wishes to see written in the Gospel the wonderful and the special love that our Lord had for her, personifying as she does all the habitual sinners who have been truly converted and called to the grace of contemplation, he shall find that our Lord would not allow any man or woman, yes, even her own sister, to speak a word against her, unless he answered on her behalf. And what's more, he reproached Simon the Leper in his own house, because he entertained hostile thoughts about her.* This was great love; this was surpassing love.

* cf Matthew 28:1–8 and John 20:11–13. 'Simon the Leper': Mark 14:3.

CHAPTER 23

*How God will answer and provide for those who, immersed in
contemplation, may not answer or provide for themselves.*

If we will eagerly conform our love and our way of life, as far as lies
in us by virtue of grace and spiritual advice, to Mary's love and her
way of life, no doubt he shall answer in the same way now for us,
spiritually and intimately, each day, in the hearts of all those that
either speak or entertain thoughts against us. As happened with
Mary, there will always be some people that speak or entertain
thoughts against us, while we are occupied with the hard work of
this life. We will behave as she did: pay no more attention to their
speeches, or to their thoughts, and not leave off our spiritual,
intimate work on account of their words and their thoughts. If
those who speak and think thus do so benevolently, our Lord shall
answer them in spirit, so that within a few days they will feel
ashamed of their words and their thoughts.

As he will answer in spirit on our behalf, so will he motivate
other men to give us the necessities of life, such as food and
clothing and other things, if he sees that we are not willing to
abandon our contemplation simply because of concern with them.
I say this in order to confute the error of those who say that it is
not lawful for men to dedicate themselves to serve God in the
contemplative life, unless they possess their bodily necessities
outright beforehand. They say that 'God helps those who help
themselves'. They speak inaccurately about God, as they well
know. Trust steadfastly, whoever you are that truly turn from the
world to God, that God shall send you one of two things, without
your having to work for it: that is, either an abundance of material
necessities, or physical strength and spiritual patience with which
to bear privation. Why should someone care about which it is that
he has? To true contemplatives, these things are all the same in the
end. If anyone doubts this, either the devil is in his breast and is
removing the belief from him, or else he has not yet properly
turned towards God, however subtly he argues about it, and

notwithstanding the pious reasons that he puts forth about this matter, whoever he is.

So, if you dedicate yourself to be contemplative, as Mary was, choose rather to be humbled under the wonderful loftiness and worthiness of God, who is perfect, than under your own wretchedness, which is imperfect: that is to say, take care that your special attention is directed more to the worthiness of God than to your wretchedness. Those who are perfectly humbled shall have no physical or spiritual needs, because they have God, who is everything; and, as this book witnesses, whoever has him needs nothing else in this life.

CHAPTER 24

*What charity is, and how it is sweetly and
perfectly encapsulated in contemplation.*

Humility is subtly and perfectly contained in this little imageless
impulse of love, when it is beating upon the dark cloud of
unknowing, with all other matters repressed and forgotten; and all
other virtues, and charity in particular, are also contained in it.

'Charity' means nothing other than love of God for himself
above all creation, and love of others as we love ourselves. It seems
good and proper that, in this work, God is loved for himself and
above all creation. The essence of this work is nothing other than
pure concentration directly aimed at God alone. I call it pure
concentration because in this work a perfect apprentice requests
neither the lessening of pain nor an increase in reward, nor (to put
it briefly) anything but God himself, to the extent that he neither
cares nor pays attention to whether he is in pain or bliss, as long as
the will of Him whom he loves be done. In this work, God is
perfectly loved for himself, and above all creation. In this work a
perfect contemplative may not allow awareness even of the holiest
creature that God ever made to interfere with his concentration.

It can also be proved that the second and lower branch of charity
to your fellow-Christian is truly and perfectly fulfilled through
contemplation, because in this work a perfect labourer has no
special attachment to anyone in particular, whether they be related
to him or not, friend or enemy. For all men seem to him to be his
kindred. He regards all men as his friends, and none as his foes, to
the extent that he thinks that all who torment him and cause him
difficulties in this life are his special friends, and thinks that he is
impelled to wish as many good things for them as he would for his
closest friend.

CHAPTER 25

The perfect contemplative feels no special
attachment to anyone else.

I am not saying that in contemplation he shall feel a special attachment to anyone living, whether friend or foe, related or unrelated. That cannot be permitted if this work is to be carried out perfectly, as when all things under God are wholly forgotten, which is necessary in contemplation. I do say, however, that he shall be made so virtuous and so charitable by contemplation that when he descends from its heights to communicate with or pray for his fellow-Christian, his will is not distracted from contemplation, for that would be a great sin. Instead, it is detached from the loftiness of this work, which is necessary and profitable because of the occasional demands of charity, and is directed as precisely towards the needs of his foe as to those of his friend (and sometimes more), and as much towards a stranger as to his relation.

Nevertheless, in this work, he has no leisure in which to consider who his friends or his enemies are, which are strangers and which his relatives. I only say that he shall sometimes (even very often!) feel a more intimate affection towards one person, or two people, or three, than to all others; and that is lawful for many reasons, as charity requires, because Christ felt this kind of intimate affection for John and Mary and Peter above many others. When he is absorbed in contemplation, however, all shall be equally intimate to him, for he shall then feel no cause except God alone, so that all shall be loved openly and purely for God's sake, as well as God in himself.

All people were lost through Adam's sin, and all who are willing show in their works their desire for salvation. Just as they are, and shall be, saved by the sole virtue of Christ's Passion, so in an analogous way someone who is perfectly immersed in this work, and united with God in spirit, as experience shows, does his best to make all men as perfect as he is. For just as when one of our limbs feels sore, all the other limbs ache and are similarly uncomfortable, or, if a limb feels healthy, all the rest are relieved by this, so is it the case spiritually with all the 'limbs' of Holy Church. If we are in a state of charity, Christ is the head, and we are the limbs; and whoever wishes to be a perfect disciple of our Lord should strain his spirit at this spiritual work, for the salvation of all his brothers and sisters, as our Lord did his body on the cross. He does not do this just for his friends, relations and intimate companions, but for all mankind in general, without any particular attachment to anyone in particular. All who wish to abandon sin and ask for mercy shall be saved through the virtue of his Passion.

What has been said here concerning humility and charity should be similarly understood in relation to all other virtues, because they are all intricately bound up in this little motion of love which I have already discussed.

CHAPTER 26

*Without special grace or habitual experience of common grace,
contemplation would be a truly laborious task. The
respective contributions made by God and the
soul in the work of contemplation.*

Work steadfastly, therefore, and strike at this high cloud of unknowing, and rest afterwards. Anyone who applies himself to this
work shall have to do a certain amount of hard work. What's more,
it will be very hard labour unless he experiences special grace, or
else has worked hard at this for a long time.

What makes it hard work? Certainly, not that devout impulse of
love that is continually brought about in the will, not by the
contemplative himself but by the hand of Almighty God, who is
always ready to perform this work in each soul that is disposed
towards it, and who does his best, and has done for a long time
already, in order to perform this work. So what kind of work is it?
Well, all of this work consists of repressing one's awareness of
everything that God ever made, and in keeping it under the cloud
of forgetting, which I mentioned before. This is all of it, for this is
the work of mankind, carried out with the help of grace. And the
other phenomenon mentioned above – that is to say, the impulse
of love – is the work of God alone. Therefore, perform your work,
and surely, I promise you, he will not fail you in that.

Press on, then, steadfastly: let's see how you conduct yourself.
Do you not see how he stands and waits for you? For shame! Work
hard for just a short period, and you shall soon be relieved of the
enormity and the severity of this work, for although in the
beginning, when you have no devotion, it is hard and exacting,
afterwards, when you do have devotion, what was once very hard
will be made very restful and easy for you, and you shall have either
little or no work. For then God will sometimes work all by himself:
not forever, nor yet for a long time at a stretch, but as and when it
pleases him. Then you will think it a joyful thing to do this.

Sometimes, perhaps, he will send out a beam of spiritual light, piercing this cloud of unknowing that is between you and him, and show you something of his innermost being, about which no one may speak. Then you will feel your affection enflamed with the fire of his love, far more than I could ever tell you. For I dare not take it upon myself to speak with my blabbering mortal tongue about the work that is God's responsibility alone: and, to put it briefly, even if I dared, I would not be willing to do it. I am fully prepared, however, to tell you about the work that is man's responsibility, when he feels himself stirred and helped by grace, for there is less risk in discussing this.

CHAPTER 27

Who should perform this work of grace.

First and foremost, I will tell you who should work at contemplation, and when, and by what means, and what kind of moderation you must display in it. If you were to ask me who should work in this way, I would nominate all who have sincerely abandoned the world and, to this end, have devoted themselves to the contemplative life rather than the active. Whoever they are, and whether or not they have been habitual sinners, all such people should labour in this work of grace.

CHAPTER 28

*No one should presume to engage in this work before his conscience
has been lawfully cleansed from all his sinful deeds.*

If you ask me when they should work at this activity, I would
stipulate that this should not happen before their conscience has
been cleansed from all the particular sins that they committed
beforehand, in accordance with the laws of Holy Church.

In contemplation, a soul dries up the root and foundation of sin
that will always live in it after confession, no matter how diligent
it is. Therefore, whoever wishes to labour at this work should first
cleanse his conscience: and then, when he has done his best to
achieve this, let him address himself courageously but humbly to
the work. He should think, moreover, that he has been held back
from it for a long time, for this is the work in which he would
have laboured throughout his life, even if he had not committed
mortal sin.

As long as a soul inhabits this mortal flesh, it shall always see and
feel this cumbersome cloud of unknowing between it and God.
Not only that, but in the torment of original sin, it shall always see
and feel that some of God's creatures, or some of their activities,
will keep intruding into his consciousness and interposing themselves between him and God. This is the righteous judgement of
God, because when man had sovereignty and lordship over all
other creatures, he wilfully turned himself into their subject,
abandoning the commandment of God, his creator. Now, when
he wishes to fulfil God's commandment, he sees and feels that all
the creatures that should be beneath him proudly throng above
him, between him and his God.

CHAPTER 29

*One should work diligently at contemplation, endure the pain
resulting from it, and judge no one.*

Anyone who desires to achieve the purity that he lost through sin,
and to win through to that state of spiritual wealth in which all
sorrow has disappeared, must continually labour at this work, and
put up with all the pain arising from it. This is the case whoever he
is, and whether or not he has been a habitual sinner.

Everyone, sinners and comparative innocents alike, finds this
hard work. It is an indisputable fact, however, that those that have
been sinners have a greater task than those that have not. Nevertheless, it often happens that some people, who have been terrible
and habitual sinners, attain perfection sooner than those that have
not. This is the merciful miracle of our Lord, who specially sends
his grace, to the wonder of the whole world. I truly believe that at
Judgement Day, when God and his gifts shall be seen clearly,
justice will be done. Then it shall be seen that some, who are now
despised and valued lightly, or not at all, because they are common
sinners, and perhaps some that are now terrible sinners, will sit with
the saints in the sight of God, most fittingly; whereas some that
now seem very holy and are worshipped by men as angels are, and
perhaps some that never yet committed deadly sins, shall sit very
sorrowfully among the devils.

Through this example you may appreciate that in this life no
man should be judged by another simply because of the good or
evil that he has done. The dead may be lawfully judged, but not
living men, whether good or evil.

CHAPTER 30

Who has the right to blame or reprove the faults of others?

Who, therefore, shall judge men's deeds? Those who have the power over and care of their souls, whether this is given openly by the laws of Holy Church, or else privately, by a special impulse from the Holy Spirit in perfect charity. Each man should take care that he does not presume to take it upon himself to blame and reprove other men's faults, unless he truly feels that he has been stirred within by the Holy Spirit: otherwise, he may very easily be mistaken in his judgements. Therefore, take care: judge yourself as you wish, in the presence of God or of your spiritual adviser, and leave other people alone.

CHAPTER 31

Anyone beginning contemplation must guard himself
against all sinful thoughts and tendencies:

After you have done your best legitimately to make amends
according to the stipulation of Holy Church, you must swiftly
turn your attention to this work. If memories of old sins, or
intimations of new ones, keep thronging into your mind and
getting between you and God, step steadfastly over them with a
fervent impulse of love, and stamp them down under foot.
Resolve to cover them with a thick cloud of forgetting, as if they
had never been committed by you or anyone else. Repress them as
often as they rise up. If this work seems difficult to you, you can
discover tactics and manoeuvres and secret spiritual techniques in
order to discard them; and such intricate arts are better learned
from God through experience than from any teacher in this life.

CHAPTER 32

Spiritual resources helpful for someone beginning contemplation.

Nevertheless, to the best of my understanding. I shall tell you something about these techniques. Put what I say to the test, and improve on it if you can.

Do your best to behave as if you do not know that they press so hard upon you, getting between you and God. Behave as if you were looking over their shoulders, looking for something else, which is God, enclosed in a cloud of unknowing. If you behave like this, I believe that within a short time you shall receive relief from your hard work. If properly understood, this tactic is nothing other than a longing for God, a desire to feel and see him as far as this is possible in this life. Such a desire is a manifestation of charity, and always deserves to incur such relief.

There is another tactic: test it out if you wish. When you feel that you cannot beat them down, cower under them like a captive and a coward overcome in battle, and consider it foolish to contend any longer with them: in such a way, you yield to God in the hands of your enemies, and feel as if you had been overcome for ever. Pay good attention to this tactic, I beg you: for it seems to me that when you try it out, your enemies will melt into thin air. If properly understood, this technique is nothing other than true self-knowledge and an unsparing awareness of yourself as you are – a filthy wretch, far worse than nothing – and this knowledge and awareness constitute humility. Such humility is rewarded by God himself mightily descending to avenge you on your enemies, and to take you up and tenderly dry your spiritual eyes, as a father does with a child that is on the point of being slaughtered in the mouth of wild swine or mad, snarling bears.

CHAPTER 33

*The contemplative is cleansed both of his sins and of the pain
produced by them. How there is still no perfect rest in this life.*

I will not describe any more techniques for you at this point: if you
have grace to test these out, I believe that you will better be able to
teach me than I you. Although I should be able to teach you, I truly
think that I am very far from that stage. Therefore, I implore you,
help me, and try this out for your sake and mine.

Press on, then, and work hard for now, I beg you: and if you
can't immediately put these tactics into practice, suffer the pain
with humility. Truly, this is your purgatory. When your torment
has passed, and your techniques are supplied by God and become
habitual through grace, then I have no doubt that you are cleansed
not only from sin but also from the pain of sin. I am referring to the
pain of your particular sins committed beforehand, and not to the
pain of original sin, because no matter how diligent you are, that
particular pain will always hurt you until you die. It will only afflict
you slightly in comparison with the torment from your particular
sins, and yet you shall not lack hard work, because new, fresh sinful
impulses will always arise from this original sin, and you must
always smite them down, and be busy to shear them away with a
sharp, double-edged sword of temperance. By this you may see
and learn that there is no true security and no true rest in this life.

Nevertheless, you must not retreat from this point, nor yet be
inordinately afraid of failure. If you have the grace to destroy the
torment from your particular sins – in the aforesaid manner, or in
a better way if you can manage it – you may be certain that the
torment of original sin, or the stirrings of new sins, will only be able
to afflict you slightly.

CHAPTER 34

*God gives this grace freely and directly, and it may
not be obtained by indirect means.*

If you ask me how you are to start this work, I beseech Almighty
God, of his great grace and great courtesy, to teach you himself, for
truly I cannot tell you. There's little surprise in that, because this is
the work of God alone, deliberately wrought in whichever soul he
pleases, without the individual's having deserved it. Without
God's help, no saint or angel could think about desiring it. I believe
that our Lord will undertake as deliberately and as often – yes! and
more deliberately and more often than this – to perform this work
in those that have been habitual sinners than in those who,
comparatively speaking, never caused him great unhappiness. He
wishes to do this, because he wishes to be seen as All-merciful and
Almighty, and because he wishes to be seen to work as, where and
when he pleases.

Yet he does not grant his grace, or perform this work in any soul
that is unable to withstand it. Whether it is the soul of a sinner or
of an innocent, no one capable of receiving this grace goes without
it. It is not given because of innocence, or withheld because of sin.
Pay attention to the fact that I say 'withheld', not 'withdrawn'.
Take care not to make a mistake here, I beg you, because the
nearer men are to the truth, the more careful they need to be of
falling into error. I only mean well. If you can't make sense of it,
leave it be until God comes and teaches you. Do this, and don't
torment yourself.

Beware of pride, because it blasphemes God's gifts, and embold-
ens sinners. If you were truly humble, you would share my attitude
towards this work and think that God gives it freely without any
merit on the part of the individual. The condition of this work is
such that its presence enables a soul to possess and feel it. No soul
may have that ability without it. The ability to perform this work is
part and parcel of the work itself, so that whoever feels drawn to
contemplation is able to do it, and otherwise not, to the extent that

without this work a soul is (as it were) dead, and cannot yearn after it. You have it to the extent that you wish for it, no more and no less; yet it is not will, nor any desire, but something else – you never know what – that stirs you to wish and desire for that thing – you never know what. Don't worry if you know no more than this, I beg you: but keep going, so that you are always progressing.

To put it more accurately, let that thing have its way with you and lead you wherever it likes. Be passive and let it be active: just look at it, and leave it alone. Do not interfere with it, as if you wished to assist it, in case you upset everything. Just be the wood, and let it be the carpenter; be the house, and let it be the householder who occupies it. Be blind during this time and shear away the desire for knowledge, for it will hinder you more than help you. It suffices that you should feel yourself lovingly stirred with something – you never know what, except that in your stirring you have no particular thought about anything beneath God, and that your concentration is directed purely at God.

If this is the case, trust steadfastly that it is God alone, without any other means either on his part or yours, that stirs your will and your desire. Do not be afraid of the devil, for he may not come so near. Only occasionally may he come to stir a man's will, and then at some remove, no matter how crafty a devil he is. No good angel can stir your will adequately without some means. Nor, to put it briefly, can anything except God.

You may understand partially through these observations, but much more clearly by testing them in practice, that men must use no indirect methods in contemplation. All good methods depend upon it, not the other way round; none may contribute to it.

CHAPTER 35

Three practices which should occupy an apprentice in the
contemplative life: reading, thinking, and praying.

Nevertheless, there are methods with which an apprentice
contemplative should be occupied, and they are as follows: the
lesson, meditation and prayer, otherwise known to you as reading,
thinking and praying. You will find a much better discussion of
them than any I can offer in another man's work,* and therefore it
is not necessary here to tell you about their particularities. I can tell
you this, though: these three are so joined together, that for
beginners and the more advanced – but not those that are virtually
perfect – thinking may not be properly achieved without reading or
listening beforehand. Reading and listening are all part of the same
process: priests read books and lay men 'read' priests when they hear
them preach the word of God. No prayer may be properly achieved
by beginners and more advanced practitioners unless thinking
precedes it. You can prove this by experience.

Whether written or spoken, God's word is like a mirror. In a
spiritual sense, the eye of your soul is your reason; you conscience
is your spiritual countenance. Just as, when there is a foul blemish
on your face, your physical eye cannot see that spot, nor discover
it, without a mirror or some source of information beyond itself, so
it is in the spiritual sense. Without reading or hearing God's word,
it is inconceivable to man's understanding that a soul that has been
blinded by habitual sin should see the foul spot on its conscience.
So it follows that only when a man sees in a physical or spiritual
mirror, or learns from other men, where the foul spot (whether
physical or spiritual) is on his face, does he run to the well to wash
himself. If the spot is a specific sin, then the well is Holy Church,
and the water is confession, with all its attendant circumstances. If

* 'Another man's work': possibly a reference to the first book of Walter
Hilton's *Scale of Perfection*. See also a similar reference in chapter 48.

it is only a blind root and stirring of sin, then the well is merciful God, and the water prayer, and all that goes with it.

Thus you may see that beginners and the more advanced cannot think properly without the prerequisites of reading or listening; neither may they pray properly without prior thinking.

CHAPTER 36

The meditations of habitual contemplatives.

This is not the case, however, with those who continually labour at contemplation, for their meditations take the form of sudden conceptions and imageless intimations of their own wretchedness, or of the goodness of God, without any prior reading or hearing, and without any special attachment to anything beneath God. These sudden conceptions and imageless intimations are more quickly learned from God than from man.

I do not think it important even if you now have no other meditations on your own wretchedness, or on the goodness of God — I mean if you feel yourself thus stirred by grace and by spiritual advice. You only need to meditate on the word 'sin' and the word 'God', or on some others, whatever you like — not analysing or expounding these words with a speculative intelligence, considering their grammatical quantities, as if you wished to increase your devotion by such means. That attitude is not at all suited to contemplation. Keep these words together instead, and think of sin as a lump, you don't know what precisely but nothing other than yourself. I think that in this imageless consideration of sin congealed into a lump (nothing other than itself) there is nothing madder than you should be at this time. Yet, perhaps, whoever looks on you would think you very soberly disposed, without any change in your appearance, but sitting, or walking, or lying, or leaning, or standing, or kneeling, as if you were in a profound period of rest.

CHAPTER 37

The special prayers of habitual contemplatives.

Just as the meditations of those who continually labour in the grace of contemplation rise spontaneously without any indirect means, so do their prayers. I am referring to their special prayers, not to the prayers that have been ordained by Holy Church, for true contemplatives esteem these most highly, and therefore observe the rituals that have been ordained by our holy Fathers. Their special prayers always rise swiftly to God, without any intervening methods or any particular premeditation beforehand, or simultaneously.

If they are verbal, which only happens occasionally, then they take the form of very few words, and the fewer the better. Indeed, I think a monosyllable would be better than a disyllable or a polysyllable for this work of the spirit, because a spiritual labourer in this work should always be at the highest and most sovereign spiritual peak. Nature provides a clear example of this. A person who is afraid because of a sudden outbreak of fire, or a man's death, or something else, is suddenly driven by the force of his feelings, in haste and necessity, to cry or beg for help. How does he do this? Not in many words, nor yet in long words – and why is that? Because he thinks it would take too long to explain what his immediate needs are. Therefore, he bursts out terrifyingly in great haste, and yells out a simple, monosyllabic word, such as 'Fire!' or 'Help!'

Just as this little word 'fire' stirs up and catches the attention of those who hear it more swiftly, so does a little monosyllabic word, not only when spoken or thought, but also when uttered secretly in the depths of the spirit, which is also its height (for in the spiritual life, all is one: height and depth, length and breadth). It pierces the hearing of Almighty God more than any long excerpt from the psalter mindlessly mumbled with the mouth alone. This is why it has been written that a short prayer pierces heaven.

CHAPTER 38

How and why brief prayer pierces heaven.

So, why does this little monosyllabic word pierce heaven? Because it is uttered with complete devotion, in the height and depth, and length and breadth of the spirit of the one who prays it. It is in the 'height' because it is prayed with all the power of the spirit. It is in the 'depth', because in this little syllable are contained all the faculties of the spirit. It is in the 'length', because if it were always to feel as it feels, it would always cry as it cries. It is in the 'breadth', because it wishes for all others what it wishes for itself. It is during this period that a soul has partially grasped something of the length and breadth, the height and the depth of the everlasting and all-loving, almighty and all-knowing God, just as Saint Paul and all the saints describe. The everlastingness of God is his length; his love is his breadth; his power is his height; and his wisdom is his depth. It is no wonder that a soul conformed by grace to the image and the likeness of God, his maker, is soon heard by God. This is true even if it is a very sinful soul, which is, as it were, an enemy to God. If it comes through grace to cry out such a little syllable in the height and the depth, the length and breadth of its spirit, it will always be heard and helped by God, because of the terrifying noise of this cry.

Consider this example. If someone is your deadly enemy, and you hear him sounding so afraid that he passionately yells out this little word 'Fire!' or 'Help!', without thinking about the fact that he is your enemy, but out of pure pity, stirred and animated by the bitterness of this cry, you rise up – yes, even though it is a winter's night! – and help him to put out his fire, or to calm down and rest in his illness. Ah, Lord! Since a man may be induced through grace to have so much mercy and to take so much pity on his enemy, notwithstanding his enmity, what pity and what mercy shall God, who has everything naturally which man has by grace, and much more – feel at a soul's cry, uttered in the height and the depth, the length and the breadth of the spirit? He will surely have much more mercy, without comparison, since what comes naturally to something is manifested more spontaneously than what it obtains by grace.

CHAPTER 39

How a perfect contemplative should pray. The nature of prayer and the words most suited to verbal prayer.

We must pray, therefore, in the height and the depth, the length and the breadth of our spirit, and not in many words but in a little monosyllabic word. What kind of word? Well, the kind that best suits the nature of prayer. So, what might that be? Let us first understand properly the nature of prayer, and then we may more clearly know what word will be most suitable for it.

Prayer is nothing other than a devout intention, directed at God for the obtaining of blessings and the removing of evils. Since all evils are either causally or essentially bound up in sin, when we wish deliberately to pray for the removing of evils, let us either utter or think nothing other than this little word 'sin'. If we wish deliberately to pray for the obtaining of good things, let us cry, either verbally, or with our thoughts or with our desires, using no other words than 'God', because God is all good things, both causally and essentially.

Do not be surprised that I privilege these words over all others. If I knew any shorter words that encapsulated all good things and all evils as comprehensively as these two words do, or if I had been taught by God to select any other words, I would have used them and left these alone; and so I advise you to do the same. Do not study in order to discover other words, or you will never achieve your goal, for it is achieved through grace alone, and not by studying. Therefore, although I have given you these examples, do not use any words to pray in except those that God inspires you to use. Nevertheless, if God stirs you to select these particular words, I do not advise you to leave them, because they are very short words. I am specifically referring to verbal prayer; otherwise, you do not need them.

Although I am recommending that you pray briefly, I am not advising you to pray infrequently. As I have said before, prayer is uttered in the length of the spirit, so that it shall never cease until it has fully obtained what it longed for. We have an example of this in the man or woman who is afraid, as I described above, for we see that they never stop shouting this little word 'help' or 'fire' until they have for the most part obtained relief from their trouble.

CHAPTER 40

The contemplative is not preoccupied by
any particular vice or virtue.

In the same way, fill your soul with the spiritual meaning of this word 'sin', without relating it to any particular kind of sin, whether venial or mortal: pride, wrath or envy, avarice, sloth, gluttony or lechery. What do contemplatives care about which sin it is, or how great it is? They think that all sins are of the same degree of importance (I mean while they are actually contemplating), considering that the smallest sin divides them from God, and disrupts their spiritual poise.

Feel sin as a lump of matter, you never know what, but nothing other than itself. Keep crying out in your spirit this one thing: 'Sin, sin, sin: help, help, help!' This spiritual exclamation is better learned from God by experience than taught verbally by a human teacher. It works best when it is spiritually pure, without any particular thought or specific utterance, except on that rare occasion when it bursts out into speech through sheer spiritual fervour, when body and soul are both filled with sorrow and the burden of sin.

You should behave in the same way with this little word 'God'. Fill your soul with its spiritual meaning, without any particular consideration of any of his works – whether they are good, better or best of all, whether physical or spiritual – or thought of any virtue that may be wrought in man's soul by any grace, and not paying attention whether it be meekness or charity, patience or abstinence, hope, faith and temperance, chastity or voluntary poverty. What do contemplatives care about this? They find and experience all virtues in God, for in him everything exists both causally and essentially. They think that if they had God, they would have all good things; and therefore they desire nothing in particular except God alone. You should behave in the same way, as grace allows you to progress: concentrate on God alone and only God, so that nothing is active in your understanding and in your will except God alone.

As long as you are in this wretched life, it is necessary that you always feel this foul, stinking lump of sin in some way, as if it was united and bound up with the essence of your being. Therefore, concentrate on these two words 'God' and 'Sin' alternately, bearing this general principle in mind: if you had God, you would be devoid of sin, and if you could be devoid of sin, you would then possess God.

CHAPTER 41

One should observe moderation in all
activities except contemplation.

If you were to ask me what moderation you should observe in contemplation, I would say 'None at all!' You must show moderation in all your other activities, such as eating and drinking, sleeping and protecting your body from extremes of heat and cold, and in praying or reading for long stretches or in conversations with your fellow-Christians. You must practise moderation in all these things, so that they do not assume too great or too small an importance. But you must not have any notion of moderation in relation to contemplation, for I would prefer that you never ceased from this work while you live.

I am not saying that you must persevere at it with the same continuous feeling of freshness, for that is not possible. Sometimes sickness and other unforeseen physical and spiritual upsets, and many other natural accidents, will greatly hinder you and often pull you down from the height of contemplation. You should always keep at it as a duty or as a pleasure, that is to say, either in the work itself or when it is just a good intention. So, for the love of God, take as much care as you reasonably can not to fall ill, so that you are not responsible for your own frailty. This work demands great repose, and a fresh and well-knit disposition, both physically and spiritually.

Also, for the love of God, exercise temperance in your physical and spiritual self-government, and keep as healthy as you can. If sickness comes in spite of all you can do, have patience and humbly wait for God's mercy; then everything will be satisfactory. Often, patience in sickness and other diverse tribulations pleases God more than any loving devotion that you may offer when healthy.

CHAPTER 42

Only through immoderation in contemplation may
one observe moderation in all other things.

Perhaps you will ask me how you should control yourself when
eating and sleeping and in all these other activities, and to this I
give a very short answer: 'Take it as it comes!' Always perform this
work, without ceasing, and without any sense of moderation, and
you will know how to begin and end all your other activities with
a strong sense of moderation. I do not believe that someone who
perseveres in this work night and day without moderation would
be able to go wrong in any of these outward activities, or he would
always go wrong, whatever he did.

If I could pay sharp and diligent attention to this spiritual work
within my soul, I would then be indifferent about eating and
drinking, sleeping and speaking, and all my external activities. For
certainly, I think I would rather achieve moderation in them by
this kind of detachment than through any diligent preoccupation
with those activities, as if I wished in that way to establish a
benchmark and a notion of moderation in relation to them.
Anyway, I would never manage to do this, no matter what I did or
said. Let men say what they will, and let experience prove this. Lift
up your heart with an imageless stirring of love, and concentrate
sometimes on sin and sometimes on God. It is God that you desire,
and sin that you detest. God desires you; and you are certain of
possessing sin. May good God help you now, for you need it!

CHAPTER 43

All self-consciousness must be abandoned, if one wishes to
experience the perfection of contemplation in this life.

Take care that nothing except God alone is at work in your understanding, or in your will. Try to get rid of all knowledge and feeling of anything lower than God, and tread everything very far down under the cloud of forgetting. You cannot only forget all creatures other than yourself in this work, or their deeds or yours; you must also forget yourself and the tasks you perform for God, as well as all other creatures and their actions. The condition of a perfect lover is not only to love something more than himself, but also to hate himself on account of what he loves.

This is the way you should behave towards yourself: you must detest and be wary of everything that is at work in your understanding and your will, unless it is God alone. Anything else, whatever it might be, is between you and God. No wonder you should hate to think about yourself, when you must always feel sin as a foul, stinking lump, you never know what, between you and God – a lump which is nothing other than itself. For you must think that it is united and bound up indivisibly with the essence of your being.

Destroy all knowledge and feeling about all aspects of creation, but most particularly about yourself. The former is dependent on the latter, because in comparison with your own self-consciousness, all other things are easily forgotten. If you will dutifully dedicate yourself to testing this out, you will find that when you have forgotten all other creatures and all their activities, and, indeed, all your own activities, between you and God there will still remain a raw self-consciousness which must always be destroyed before you can truly experience the perfection of contemplation.

CHAPTER 44

*How the soul must govern itself in order to destroy
the individual's self-consciousness.*

Now you ask me how you may destroy this raw self-consciousness.
Perhaps you think that if it were to be destroyed, all other
hindrances would be too; and if you think along these lines, you
are thinking in the right way. I would answer, though, that
without a very special grace freely given by God, and a
corresponding willingness on your part to receive this grace, such
self-consciousness cannot be destroyed.

A strong and profound spiritual sorrow will enable you to
achieve this, but you should exercise moderation in this sorrow, as
follows: you must take care during this period that you do not
harshly strain either your body or your spirit, but sit very still, as if
resting, exhausted with sobbing and sunk in sorrow. This is true
sorrow; this is perfect sorrow; and one who achieves this sorrow
will succeed.

All men have reasons to be sorrowful, but particularly the one
who knows and feels that he is. In comparison with this, all other
sorrows are superficial. The person who feels not only *what* he is,
but *that* he is, sorrows in earnest, and anyone who never felt this
sorrow may truly be sorrowful, because he never yet felt perfect
sorrow. When it is experienced, this sorrow cleanses the soul not
only from sin but also from the pain that it experiences because of
sin. To that end, it enables a soul to receive that joy which deprives
a man of all self-consciousness. Properly understood, this sorrow is
full of holy desire – if it were otherwise, a man could never bear the
experience of it in this life. If a soul were not nourished with a kind
of comfort resulting from its correct behaviour, it would not be able
to bear the pain that it receives from its own self-consciousness.
Every time a person wishes to have a true awareness and feeling of
God in purity of spirit, as far as is possible in this life, and feels that
he may not have this (because he is only too aware of that foul
stinking lump of himself, which must always be hated, and despised

and forsaken if he is to be God's perfect disciple and instructed by him in the mount of perfection), he nearly goes mad with sorrow, to the extent that he weeps and wails, strains, swears and curses and, to put it briefly, thinks that he carries such a heavy burden of himself that he does not care what becomes of him, just so long as God wills it. Yet, in the midst of all this sorrow, he does not wish to cease to exist, for that would be diabolical madness and an act of contempt to God. No, he very much wishes to exist, and he thanks God very fervently for the worthiness and the gift of his existence, even though he ceaselessly desires to be relieved of the burden of self-consciousness.

Each soul must experience this sorrow and this desire, either in this way or in another. God undertakes to teach his spiritual disciples according to the dictates of his benevolence and their corresponding abilities to bear it physically and spiritually, until they may be perfectly united with God in absolute charity. That may be obtained here if God grants it.

CHAPTER 45

Some misconceptions that may occur during contemplation.

I must tell you one thing: a young disciple, who has not yet been tried and tested in spiritual work, may easily be deceived and, unless he is alert and has grace to desist and to submit himself to spiritual advice, his physical powers may perhaps be undermined and his spiritual faculties may become ensnared with delusions. All this happens as a result of pride, worldliness and intellectual inquisitiveness.

Such a delusion may come about in the following manner. A young man or woman, newly dedicated to the school of devotion, hears this sorrow and this desire – how a man must lift up his heart to God, and ceaselessly desire to feel the love of God – being read about and discussed. Immediately, their speculative intelligence gets to work and they don't interpret the words in the spiritual sense, as they are intended, but in the material and literal sense, and they make their material inclinations toil appallingly in their heart, and what with the lack of grace that they incur, their pride and speculation, they strain their veins and their physical faculties so grossly and harshly that within a short period they fall into exhaustion and a kind of physical and spiritual lethargy, which makes them let themselves go and seek out some superficial material and physical comfort beyond themselves, for physical and spiritual recreation. If this plight does not overtake them, then because of their spiritual blindness and the physical inflammation that arises during the time of this fake spiritual (but in fact carnal) activity, either their breasts become inflamed with an unnatural warmth, or else they sense a dubious warmth inflicted by the devil, their spiritual enemy, aided and abetted by their pride, their material inclinations and facile speculation.

Neverthless, they may think it is the fire of love, kindled by the grace and goodness of the Holy Spirit. Much harm is caused by this deception and its ramifications: hypocrisy, heresy and a great deal of error. Hot on the heels of this fake sensation comes false knowledge obtained in the devil's school, just as after an authentic sensation one receives true instruction from the tutelage of God. For I tell you, the devil has his contemplatives, just as God does. Just like the authentic sensations and knowledge experienced by those who have been saved, this deception, involving false sensations, and consequently false knowledge, has remarkable, diverse variations, according to the differing states and conditions of those who are deceived.

I will not discuss any deceptions here other than those that I think will afflict you, should you ever decide to work at contemplation. For what good would it do you to know how important clerks, and men and women in walks of life other than yours, are deceived? None at all, surely! Therefore I will not discuss anything except those that afflict the contemplative. You must take care in your work, if you come across them.

CHAPTER 46

How one must avoid these misconceptions, and work with
a willingness of spirit rather than with any brute force.

For the love of God, take care in this work and do not put your heart
under harsh or immoderate strain; work with a good intention
rather than with any gross brute force. For the more pure your
intention, the more humble and spiritual it will be; the more brutish
your work, the more carnal and crude. So, take care, because the
carnal heart that presumes to reach the summit of this work will be
beaten away with stones. Stones are dry and hard by nature, and they
hurt very much when they strike. Such brutal efforts are harshly
associated with the carnality of physical sensation, and are very dry
because they lack the moisture of grace; and they hurt the hapless
soul very much, and make it fester in its diabolical delusions.
Therefore, beware of this gross behaviour, and teach yourself to love
vigorously with a gentle and demure bearing that is as much physical
as spiritual. Attend politely and humbly on our Lord's will, and no
matter how sharply you feel your hunger, do not snatch at it too
quickly, like a ravenous greyhound. I would coyly add that you
should do your best to restrain the clamorous and unwieldy yearning
of your spirit, as if you did not want him to know how eager you are
to see him, and possess or feel him.

You might think that this is a rather immature suggestion, but I
believe that if someone had the grace to behave and feel as I
recommend, he would be aware of God playing lovingly with him,
as a father does with his child, hugging and kissing it – and he
would enjoy the experience.

CHAPTER 47

Concerning spiritual purity. One must show one's desire
in one way to God, and in another way to man.

Do not be surprised that I speak in this playful way and in a
seemingly coy and unnaturally immoderate way. I do this for
certain reasons, and because it seems to me that I have been urged
for many days to feel, think and speak in this way, and as much to
my other special friends in God as to you.

The reason why I urge you to hide your heart's desire from God
is as follows: I think that such concealment would bring it more
clearly to his attention, to your benefit and in fulfilment of your
desire, than would any other manner of disclosure that you could
muster. There is another reason: I hope that this kind of oblique
disclosure will bring you from the carnality of physical sensation
into the purity and depth of spiritual feeling, and so onwards,
ultimately helping you to tie the spiritual knot of ardent love
between you and God, in spiritual unity and concurrence of will.

You know that God is a spirit, and if anyone wishes to be united
with him, it must be in integrity and profundity of spirit, far from
any spurious physical concern. It is true that everything is known
by God, and nothing, whether physical or spiritual, may be
concealed from him. Since he is a spirit, whatever is hidden in the
depths of the spirit is more openly known and disclosed to him
than something that is contaminated with any kind of physical
matter, for all physical things are naturally further from God than
are spiritual things. For this reason, as long as our desire is contaminated with any kind of physicality — as it is when we strain and
sweat in both body and soul — it is further from God than it would
be if it were acted upon more devoutly and more vigorously, in
sobriety and purity, and in the profundity of the spirit.

Here you may appreciate in part why I ask you in such a childish
manner to conceal the impulse of your desire from God. I am not
asking you to hide it outright, because it would be foolish to ask
you to do outright what cannot be done by any means! But I ask

you to do your best in order to hide it. Why should I make such a request? Surely, because I want you to cast it into the spiritual depths, far from any gross contamination from physicality, which would make it less of a spiritual concern, and to that extent further from God; also because I well know that the more spiritual the characteristics of your soul, the less gross it is, and the nearer to God, and the better it pleases him, and the more clearly it may be perceived by him. It is not that his sight may be clearer at any time or in any respect, for it is eternally unchangeable, but, because he is a spirit, it is more like him when it is spiritually pure.

There is another reason why I ask you to do your best to keep him from knowing. You and I, and many others like us, are so capable of understanding something which is intended spiritually in physical terms that perhaps, if I had told you to reveal your heart's impulse to God, you would have given a physical manifestation of it to him, either in your demeanour, or vocally, or verbally, or through some other crude physical effort, as when you have to reveal a secret to an ordinary person. Your work would have been impure in this respect, because things must be revealed in one way to a man, and in another way to God.

CHAPTER 48

*God wishes to be served both physically and spiritually, and
will reward men in both ways. How men shall know when
all the sweet consolations that the body experiences during
the time of prayer are good, and when evil.*

I do not say this because I want you to delay if you are stirred to
pray verbally, or to cry out, because of the welling-up of devotion
in your spirit, to speak to God as if to a man, and to say something
good, such as: 'Good Jesus! Fair Jesus! Sweet Jesus!' and other
things like this. No, God forbid that you should think this! That's
not what I mean, and God forbid that I should put asunder what he
has joined together: the body and the spirit. For God wishes to be
served with body and soul, both together, as is fitting, and he gives
man his just deserts in both physical and spiritual bliss.

As a foretaste of that reward, sometimes he will enflame the body
of his devout servant here in this life – not once or twice, but
perhaps very often, as it pleases him – with remarkable delights and
comforts. Some of these do not come from outside the body,
entering it through the windows of our faculties, but from within,
rising and springing from the abundance of spiritual joy, and from
true devotion in the spirit. Such a comfort and such a delight must
not be regarded with suspicion; and, to put it briefly. I think that
whoever feels it does not regard it in this way.

I beg you, though, to regard with suspicion all other comforts,
noises, feelings of gladness, delights, that come suddenly from
beyond you, you do not know whence. For they may be both
good and evil, brought about by a good angel if they are good and
otherwise by an evil angel. This may be no bad thing if the
delusions of the speculative intelligence and of the disorderly
efforts of your corporeal heart are laid to one side, as I advise you
(or as you may learn better yourself). Why is that? Because of this
comfort, that is to say, the devout impulse of love that inhabits the
pure spirit. This is brought about by the hand of Almighty God,
without any intermediary, and therefore it must always be far from

any delusion, or any false notion that a man may pick up in this life.

I think I won't tell you at this stage how you may discern whether other comforts, sounds and delights are good or evil, because I don't think it's necessary. You may find it written about in another man's work, and a thousand times better than I can put it, and such may be the case with what I will discuss here, too. But so what? I shan't abandon it, and it won't annoy me to fulfil the desire and the longing of your heart, which you have revealed to me, first in your words and now in your deeds.

But I may say this much to you about the sounds and the delights that enter by the windows of your faculties, and which may be both good and evil: get used to this imageless, devout and vigorous stirring of love that I am telling you about. I have no doubt that it will enable you to discriminate between them. If you are partly stunned by them on the first occasion, because they are unfamiliar to you, your devotion will bind your heart so tightly that it will not give them full credence before you receive either inward assurance about them from the spirit of God, or outward assurance from the advice of a spiritual adviser.

CHAPTER 49

The essence of all perfection is nothing other than a
good will; and how all consolations that may
occur in this life are only incidental.

Therefore, I beg you, attend devotedly to this humble stirring of
love in your heart, and follow it, because it will be your guide in
this life, and will bring you to bliss in the next. It is the essence of
all good living, and without it no good work may be begun or
completed. It is nothing other than a good will, directly corresponding to that of God, and a kind of full satisfaction and a
gladness that you feel in your will because of all that he does.

This kind of good will is the essence of all perfection. No matter
how holy they are, all delights and comforts, whether physical or
spiritual, are simply extraneous in comparison with this. They are
merely dependent on this good will. I describe them as inessential
because they may be experienced and lost without the will itself
being affected. That is what happens in this life, but not in the bliss
of heaven, for there they will be indivisibly united with their
essence as shall the body, in which they work, with the soul; so
their essence here is only a good spiritual will. I firmly believe that
anyone who feels the perfection of this will (as far as it may be
experienced here) is as glad and willing to be deprived of any
delight or any comfort as he would be to feel and experience these
things, if God so wished.

CHAPTER 50

*What chaste love is; and how such consolations are given only
rarely in some cases, and very often in others.*

We should direct all our attention to this humble impulse of love in our will. If I may say so tactfully, we should care a little bit less about all other delights and comforts, physical or spiritual, no matter how attractive or holy they are. If they come, welcome them, but do not care too much about them for fear of your own frailty, because it would ask a great deal of your powers to entertain such sweet sensations and floods of tears for any long period of time. You may, perhaps, be stirred to love God in order to have them. You will know if this is the case if you complain too much when they are absent. If this happens, your love is not yet chaste or perfect. For if someone experiences chaste, perfect love, even if he allows the body to be nourished and comforted while it is experiencing such sweet sensations and outbursts of weeping, he does not begrudge it if he has to be deprived of them at God's will, but is, on the contrary, equally satisfied with that outcome.

Some people often experience such comforts, whereas others rarely experience them. All this is in accordance with what God has disposed and ordained, depending entirely on the different needs of his creatures. For some are so weak and tender in spirit that unless they are somewhat comforted by feeling such delight, they would not be able to put up with the different temptations and tribulations that they suffer and labour under in this life, from their physical and spiritual enemies. There are others who are so physically weak that they cannot perform any harsh penance whereby to cleanse themselves. Our Lord will cleanse these creatures in spirit through grace, by sweet sensations and periods of weeping. On the other hand, there are some creatures that are so spiritually strong that they may obtain sufficient comfort by offering up this reverent and humble impulse of love and concurrence of will, and do not greatly need to be nourished with such sweet comforts in the form of physical sensations. God knows, not I, which of these types is the holier and the more precious to him.

CHAPTER 51

Something that is meant spiritually should not be interpreted literally; this particularly affects the words 'in' and 'up'.

Therefore, address yourself humbly to this meek impulse of love in your heart. I do not refer to your physical heart, but to your spiritual heart, which is your will. Take good care that you do not interpret in physical terms something that is intended spiritually, because the gross, corporeal understanding of those who have speculative and ingenious intellects are the cause of much error.

You can see an example of this in my urging you to conceal your desire from God, to the best of your ability. For, perhaps, if I had urged you to reveal your desire to God, you would have understood this in more physical terms than you do now, because you well know that everything that is voluntarily concealed is cast into the depths of the spirit. Thus it seems to me that it is very necessary to have proper warnings about the interpretation of words that are intended in the spiritual sense, so that you do not understand them in the literal sense. It is particularly good to be careful with this word 'in' and this word 'up', because it seems to me that those who are determined to be contemplatives experience much error and self-deception through their misunderstanding of these two words. I know something about this by experience, and something by hearsay, and it is my intention to say a little about these kinds of self-deception.

I put the case to you of a young disciple under God's tutelage, newly withdrawn from the world, who thinks that for a brief period of time he has given himself over to penance and prayer, and who thinks, according to advice that he receives in confession, that he is therefore capable of dedicating himself to spiritual labour, about which he has heard men around him speaking or reading, or has perhaps read himself. When he reads about spiritual labour, or hears it discussed, and particularly hears about this aspect, whereby a man must draw all his faculties within himself, or how he must climb above himself eagerly (because of the blindness of the soul and the coarseness and speculative nature of natural understanding), he misunderstands these words, and thinks, because he discovers in himself a natural appetite for recondite matters, that he is therefore called to that work by grace. If his spiritual adviser does not agree with this, he immediately feels resentful towards his adviser, and thinks – yes, and perhaps even says aloud to someone in a similar position – that he cannot find anyone who properly understands him. Because of his audacity and presumption, which come from his inquisitive mind, he immediately abandons humble prayer and penance far too quickly, and applies himself (as he reckons) to proper spiritual labour in his soul. Yet, if accurately understood, this work is neither properly physical nor spiritual labour, and, to put it briefly, it is an unnatural kind of work, in which the devil is his foreman. It is the quickest route to both physical and spiritual death, because it is a form of mania, rather than wisdom, and leads a man straight to insanity. Yet he cannot see this, because he is determined to think about nothing but God.

CHAPTER 52

How young, presumptuous disciples misunderstand the word
'in', and the misconceptions that follow from this.

The insanity that I am describing is brought about in the following
manner. He reads and hears it discussed that he should abandon the
use of his outward faculties, and work inwardly; and because he
does not know what inward working is, he does it incorrectly,
because he turns his physical faculties inwards in an unnatural
manner, and strains himself, as if he wished to see inwards with his
physical eyes, and to hear inwards with his ears, and so forth in
relation to all his faculties – smelling, tasting and 'touching'
inwardly. In this way he behaves contrary to the workings of
nature, and by means of his ingenuity he strains his imagination so
excessively that he ultimately has a nervous breakdown. The devil
immediately has power to fake some spurious lights or sounds,
sweet smells in his nose, wonderful tastes in his mouth, and many
elaborate sensations of heat and burning in his chest or in his
bowels, in his back and loins, and in his private parts.

Yet, in this delusion, he thinks that he has a calm conception of
God without any hindrance from vain thoughts, and, in a sense, he
does have this, because he is so filled with lies that vanity cannot
harm him. Why? Because that same fiend who would bring vain
thoughts to him if he was working well, is the chief performer of
this work, and you can be sure that *he* won't stand in his own way.
He won't distract the man from concentrating on God, lest he
should attract suspicion towards himself.

CHAPTER 53

Various unpleasant consequences that befall those who engage
in improper modes of contemplation.

In contrast with those who are God's true disciples, who are always decorous in their physical and spiritual behaviour, those that are deceived by this false work exhibit some extraordinary behaviour. If anyone saw them when they are sitting down at this time with their eyes open, he would see them stare as if insane, and look hysterical, as if they saw the devil. Indeed, it is good to take extreme care here, for the devil is certainly not far away. Some roll back their eyes into their heads, as if they were dazed sheep that have been beaten on the head, and are about to die. Others hang their heads on one side, as if they had a worm in their ears. Some squeak instead of speaking, as if there were no spirit in their bodies. This is the true condition of the hypocrite. Some cry and make whining noises, because they are too hasty and desperate to say what they think, and that is the condition of heretics, and of those who will always be in error because of their presumption and ingenious minds.

Anyone who saw all this would appreciate that this error results in much disorderly and indecorous behaviour. Nevertheless, there are some who are so devious that they can for the most part refrain from behaving like this when they are in company, although if these men could be seen in private, I don't think they could keep it a secret. Nevertheless, I still think that if anyone were to contradict their opinion directly, he would soon see them explode in some manner – and yet they think that everything they do is for the love of God and for the upholding of truth. I truly think that unless God in a merciful miracle makes them desist immediately, they will 'love' God in this way for so long that they will go, stark staring mad, to the devil. The devil has no more perfect servant in this life than someone who is deceived and infected by all the delusions that I mention here. It may be the case that one, and possibly many, may be infected with them all. But I declare that he does not have a perfect hypocrite or heretic on this earth who is not guilty of at least some of the things I have already mentioned, or perhaps may discuss further, if God permits.

For some men are so preoccupied by the niceties of physical display that when they have to listen to anything, they twist their heads elaborately to one side, and raise their chins; their mouths gape open as if they were using them to listen with, instead of their ears. When others have to speak, they point with their fingers, or on their fingers, or on their own breasts, or on the breasts of their interlocutors. Some can neither sit still, stand still, nor lie still unless they are either twitching their feet or doing something with their hands. Some wave their arms about when they are speaking, as if they had to swim over a great expanse of water. Some are always grinning and tittering with every word that they utter, as if they were giggling idiots who didn't know how to behave. A more decorous way of behaving would be to maintain a calm and modest demeanour, with a pleasant expression.

I am not saying that all these indecorous ways of behaving are great sins in themselves, nor yet that all who perform them are great sinners. But I am saying that if such unseemly and disorderly ways of behaving control the man who exhibits them, then they are signs of pride and speculative intelligence, and of an unruly ostentation and greed for knowledge. In particular, they are authentic signs of mental instability, and also of the fact that such people have not been engaged in proper contemplation. This is the only reason why I have set down so many of these deceptions in my writing: a contemplative can then test the quality of his work with reference to them.

CHAPTER 54

How contemplation makes the individual wise and
both physically and spiritually beautiful.

When someone contemplates, it governs his body and soul very
fittingly, and makes him a favourable sight to each man or woman
who looks at him, to the extent that even if the least prepossessing
man or woman alive should come by grace to work at contemplation, their appearance would suddenly be changed through that
grace, so that each good person who saw them would be eager and
joyful to share their company, and would think that he had been
spiritually renewed and helped towards God by grace in their
presence.

Therefore, let anyone who may obtain this gift through grace do
so – for whoever truly has it shall properly govern himself and all
his affairs because of it. He would be able to distinguish, should the
need arise, between people with different kinds of characters. He
would be able to blend in with everyone who talked to him,
whether or not they were habitual sinners, without any sin in
himself, to the wonder of all who saw him; and would be able to
draw others, by the help of grace, to the same spiritual work at
which he labours.

His appearance and his words would be full of spiritual wisdom,
full of fire and fruitfulness, spoken in mature truth, without any
falsehood, and far from any pretensions or the bleating of hypocrites. There are some who, with all their inner and outer powers,
imagine how, by virtue of their conversation, they may
strengthen their own position, and buttress themselves against a
fall, with many 'unassuming', whispered words and much devout
behaviour, paying more attention to seeming holy in the sight of
men than really to be so in the sight of God and his angels.
Because of this, these people will expend more attention and
more grief over disorderly behaviour, or something tactless or
indecorous blurted out in company, then they do over the
thousand vain thoughts and stinking sinful impulses which afflict

them, or which they carelessly manifest in the sight of God and the saints and angels in heaven. Oh, Lord God! Whether or not there is as much pride within as there are so many humble, whispered words, I would agree that it is fitting and proper for those who are inwardly humble to speak with humility, and display a meek and decorous countenance outwardly, in accordance with the humility that is in their heart. I do not say, though, that this should be manifested in broken or squeaky voices, in direct contradiction with their true nature. If what they have to say is authentic, it will be delivered honestly and authoritatively, in a manner redolent of the spirit of the speaker. If anyone who naturally has a direct and loud voice speaks indistinctly and squeakily — I mean unless he is physically ill, or unless it is a private matter between him and God or his confessor — then it is a true sign of hypocrisy, whether in a young or an old person.

What more can I say about these poisonous deceptions? Well, unless they have grace to desist from such noxious hypocrisy, between that secret pride in their hearts and such 'humble' words sent forth into the world, the hapless soul may very soon sink into wretchedness.

CHAPTER 55

Those who reprove sin fervently and tactlessly are wrong.

The devil will deceive some men in this manner: he will remarkably enflame their intentions to keep God's law, and to destroy sin
in all other men. He will never tempt them with anything obvi-
ously evil. He makes them like zealous bishops, keeping watch
over all the degrees of Christian life, as an abbot does over his
monks. They will rebuke all men for their faults, just as if they had
the cure of their souls. They think that they dare not behave
otherwise, because of God, and describe the faults that they can
see, and say that they have been moved to do this by the fire of
charity, and of God's love in their hearts. In fact they are lying,
because it is the fire of hell rising up in their brains and in their
imaginations.

The truth of this may be seen from the consequences. The devil is
a spirit, and does not naturally have a body any more than an angel
does. Nevertheless, sometimes he or an angel may, with God's
permission, assume a physical shape in order to minister to any man
in this life, and the shape that he assumes suits the task he has to
perform. We have an example of this in the Bible. Whenever any
angel was sent in physical form, in both Old and New Testaments,
it was always made plain, either by his name or by one of his physical
attributes, what his spiritual concern or message was. It is the same
way with the devil, because, when he appears physically, he gives a
sign by some aspect of his outward appearance of what his servants
are in spirit.

There is one supreme example of this, which I have gleaned
from some necromancers, who have the knowledge to summon
evil spirits, and others to whom the devil has appeared in bodily
form. In whatever form the devil appears, he always has only one
nostril, and it is a great, wide one. He will gladly flare it, so that a
man may see through it up to his brain, which is nothing other
than the fire of hell, because the devil may not have another sort of
brain. If he could make a man glance in at it, he could wish for

nothing better, because, upon looking at it, anyone might be driven out of his mind forever. But an experienced necromancer knows this well enough, and can prepare properly for it, so that it does not affect him.

This is why I say that always, whenever the devil assumes any physical shape, he indicates through some aspect of his body what his servants are in spirit. For he so inflames the imagination of his contemplatives with the fire of hell that, suddenly and intemperately, they blurt out their elaborate thoughts and, without any advice, they take it upon themselves prematurely to condemn other men's faults. This is because, spiritually speaking, they have only one nostril. The septum, which is in a man's physical nose, and which divides one nostril from the other, is a sign that a man should have spiritual temperance, and should be able to separate good from evil, and evil from what is worse and the good from what is better, before he pronounces any judgement concerning anything that he hears or sees about him. In the spiritual sense, a man's brain represents his imagination, because it is naturally situated in the head, and works there.

CHAPTER 56

The self-deception of those who are more inclined towards
intellectual speculation and academic learning than
to the teaching and counsel of Holy Church.

There are some who, although not deceived with this particular kind of error, nevertheless abandon the teaching and counsel of Holy Church through pride and the inquisitiveness of the natural 'intellectual' and academic. These, with all their supporters, rely excessively on their own knowledge. Because they were never anchored in this humble, imageless sensation and virtuous way of living, they bring upon themselves a false feeling, counterfeited by their spiritual enemy, to the extent that they ultimately burst out and blaspheme all the saints, sacraments and laws of Holy Church. Worldly men, who think the laws of Holy Church too difficult to submit to, are quickly and easily drawn to these heretics and all their supporters, and if they could be seen as clearly as they will be on the last day, they would immediately appear burdened by great and horrible worldly sins and others committed in the secrecy of their foul flesh, quite apart from their blatant presumption in persevering in error. They are fittingly called the disciples of Antichrist, for it is said of them that, for all their deceptively attractive appearance, they are foul sinners in private.

CHAPTER 57

How young, presumptuous disciples misunderstand this other
word 'up'; and the misconceptions that follow from this.

Let's not say any more about that at this stage; but, to resume our
subject, let us consider how young, presumptuous spiritual disciples misunderstand this other word 'up'.

If it be the case that they either read, or hear read or discussed,
how men should lift up their hearts to God, they immediately stare
at the stars and, if they could, over the moon, and listen out for the
moment when they will hear angels singing from heaven. These
men with their restless imagination sometimes wish to pierce the
planets and make a hole in the firmament through which to look.
They make of God what they like, and clothe him richly, and set
him on a throne, far more elaborately than he was ever painted on
this earth. They will make angels with physical appearances, and
arrange them all around, playing on various instruments, more
strangely than they were ever seen or heard to do in this life.

The devil remarkably deceives some of these men, for he will
send a kind of dew – they think it is angels' food – as if it was
coming out of the air, and softly and sweetly falling into their
mouths, and therefore they grow accustomed to sitting, gaping, as
if they wanted to catch flies. Now truly, no matter how holy this
seems, it is only a deception, because at this time they have souls
that are empty of any true devotion. Much vanity and falsehood
are in their hearts, brought about by their over-elaborate labouring, to the extent that often the devil fakes fantastic noises in their
ears, delicate lights and shining in their eyes, and remarkable smells
in their noses, and it is all make-believe.

Yet they do not think so, because they think that they have an
example of this looking upwards and labouring in Saint Martin,
who in a revelation saw God clad in his mantle among his angels;
and in Saint Stephen,* who saw our Lord standing in heaven; and

* Saint Martin and Saint Stephen: Saint Martin of Tours (*c.*316–397) divided

in many others; and in Christ, who physically ascended into heaven, in the presence of his disciples. This is why they say that we should cast our eyes upwards. I agree that, in our physical observances, we should lift up our eyes and our hands as if we are moved in spirit. However, the work of our spirit must not be directed either upwards or downwards, nor to one side or the other, nor forwards or backwards, as a physical object may be. This is because our work should be spiritual, not physical, and not carried out through physical gestures.

his cloak in order to cover a beggar, and was subsequently granted a vision of Christ in heaven, wearing the half-cloak. This led to his baptism, and he eventually became Bishop of Tours. The martyrdom of Saint Stephen, who was stoned to death, is described in Acts 7:54–60.

CHAPTER 58

That no one should follow the example of Saint Martin and
Saint Stephen, straining the imagination upwards during prayer.

What they say about Saint Martin and Saint Stephen was only
manifested in a miracle, and in order to give assurance of something spiritual, even if they did see things with their bodily eyes.
For they should know that Saint Martin's mantle was never
substantially placed on Christ's own body, as if he wanted to keep
himself from the cold – but it was done by a miracle, and as an
example to who are capable of being saved, who are spiritually
united to the body of Christ, and who clothe a poor man and
perform any other good deed, physically or spiritually, for the love
of God, and for any who are needy, assured that they perform it for
Christ in the spiritual sense, and shall be rewarded as substantially
because of this as if they had done it to Christ's own body. He says
this himself in the Gospel, and yet did not consider this sufficient,
but still affirmed it afterwards by a miracle; and for this reason he
showed himself in a revelation to Saint Martin.

All the revelations that any man saw in physical form in this life
have spiritual significations, and I believe that, if those to whom
they were showed, or we for whom they were showed, had been
sufficiently spiritual, or could have understood their significations
in the spiritual sense, they would never have been manifested
physically. Therefore, let us abandon the rough bark, and nourish
ourselves on the sweet kernel.

How? Not as the heretics do – they are very like madmen in this
habit, that whenever they have drunk from a gorgeous cup, they
throw it at the wall and break it. If we wish to succeed, we must
not behave like this. We should not feed ourselves on the fruit in
such a way that we displease the tree, nor drink in such a way that
we would break the cup when we have drunk. By 'the tree' and
'the cup' I mean these visible miracles and all appropriate physical
observances that do not hinder the work of the spirit. By 'the fruit'
and 'the drink', I mean the spiritual signification of these visible

miracles, and of these appropriate physical observances, such as the lifting up of our eyes and hands to heaven. If they are done because of a spiritual impulse, then they are well done; otherwise they are false, and an aspect of hypocrisy. If they are authentic and yield spiritual fruit, why should they be despised? Men will kiss the cup because there is wine inside.

What of it if, when our Lord physically ascended into heaven, he made his way upwards into the clouds, with his mother and his disciples observing him with their bodily eyes? Should we, therefore, in our spiritual work, always stare upwards, peering after him to see if we can see him actually sitting in heaven, or else standing, as Saint Stephen saw him? He surely did not show himself physically in heaven to Saint Stephen because he wanted to set us the example that we should, in our spiritual work, look physically up to heaven in order to see him as Saint Stephen did, whether standing, or sitting, or lying down. For no man knows how his body appears in heaven – standing, sitting, or lying down – and such knowledge is not necessary. We need know no more than that his body and soul have been resurrected indivisibly. The body and the soul, which constitute his humanity, are indivisibly united with his divinity. It is not necessary to know about his sitting, standing, or lying down – except that he does as he pleases, and behaves physically as it seems most appropriate for him to do. If he shows himself lying down, or standing, or sitting, by physical revelation to anyone in this life, it is done in the interests of spiritual signification, and not on account of any physical posture that he actually adopts in heaven.

Take this example. By 'standing' you may understand an eagerness to help, and therefore one friend often says to another, when he is engaged in physical struggle: 'Keep it up, friend, and fight hard, and don't give up the struggle too easily; for I shall stand by you.' He does not only mean physical standing, for perhaps this struggle is on horseback, and not on foot, and perhaps it involves movement and not standing still. Rather, when he says that he shall 'stand by' him, he means that he will be ready to help him. It was for this reason that our Lord showed himself in physical form in heaven to Saint Stephen, when he was undergoing his martyrdom, and not to set us the example of looking up to heaven. He spoke in this way to Saint Stephen, who personifies all those who suffer persecution for the love of Christ: 'Look, Stephen! Just as I open up this physical firmament, which is called heaven, and let you see me physically standing up, trust steadfastly that I stand likewise beside you in spirit, by the power of my divinity, and I am ready to help you. Therefore, stand firmly in the faith, and courageously suffer the harsh blows from those hard stones, for I shall crown you in bliss as your reward, and not only you, but all those who in any way endure persecution for my sake.'

Thus you may see that these physical revelations were given for spiritual reasons.

CHAPTER 59

No one must adopt the physical ascension of Christ as an
example, straining the imagination upwards during
prayer. Time, place, and physical state should
be forgotten during contemplation.

If you mention the ascension of our Lord – because that was done
physically, and for a physical as well as a spiritual purpose, because
he ascended as true God and true Man – I would answer you that
he had been dead, and was clothed in immortality, and so shall we
be at the Day of Judgement. Then we shall be so subtly constituted
in both body and in soul that we shall be able to move as swiftly
with our bodies as we may now spiritually, with our thoughts,
whether up or down, on one side or another, forwards or backwards. Everything will then be equally good, as the clerks say.
Now, however, you may not approach heaven physically, but
spiritually, and such that it takes no physical form, going neither
upwards nor downwards, nor to one side or the other, backwards
or forwards.

Mark well that although all those who dedicate themselves to
spiritual labour, and particularly to contemplation, read 'lift up' or
'go in', and although this activity is referred to as a 'stirring',
nevertheless they should pay very careful attention to the fact that
this stirring up does not stretch 'up' or 'in' physically, and is not the
same kind of stirring as from one place to another. Although it is
sometimes called a 'rest', they should not think of it as the same kind
of rest as waiting in a place without moving from it. Contemplation
is so pure and so spiritual that, if properly understood, it is nothing to
do with actual stirring or any physical place.

It should rather be called a sudden change than a movement,
because time, place, and body should all be forgotten in all
contemplation. Therefore take care in this work that you do not
take as an example the physical ascension of Christ, straining your
imagination physically upwards during prayer, as if you wanted to
climb above the moon. Spiritually, it is very far from this. If you

were to ascend physically into heaven, as Christ did, then you
might take it as an example; but no one except God may do that, as
he himself showed, saying: 'There is no man that may ascend into
heaven, except the one who descended from heaven, and became
man for the love of man.'* Even if it were possible – and it really
isn't – it would take place because of spiritual work and only by the
power of the spirit, far from any physical effort or straining of our
imagination, whether upwards, or inwards, or to one side or the
other. Therefore, abandon this kind of pretence: nothing can
happen in this way.

* 'There is no man . . . love of man': John 3:13.

CHAPTER 60

That the loftiest and most direct way to heaven
is run by desires, and not by footsteps.

Now, perhaps, you are asking how this may be, since you think
that you have authentic evidence that heaven lies upwards. This is
because we believe that Christ physically ascended there, and sent
the Holy Spirit from above, as he promised, in the sight of all his
disciples. Therefore, you think, since you have proper evidence,
why should you not direct your mind physically upwards in
prayer?

I will answer this to the best of my feeble abilities: since Christ
had to ascend physically, and afterwards send the Holy Spirit in
physical form, it was more appropriate that he should ascend
upwards and send it from above, than go downwards and send it
from beneath, behind or in front, or from one side or the other. If
the concept of appropriateness didn't exist, he would never have
needed to have gone upwards rather than downwards even in
order to take the shortest route there, because heaven, when
understood spiritually, is as near 'down' as it is 'up', and vice versa,
as close behind as in front, and vice versa, and on one side as on the
other, so that anyone who had a true desire to be in heaven would
at the same time be there in spirit. For the chief and shortest route
there is taken by desires, not by footsteps. This is why Saint Paul
says of himself and many others: 'Though our bodies are at present
here on the earth, nevertheless our life is in heaven.'* He meant
love and desire, which constitute the spiritual life. A soul is truly in
the place where it loves, as it is in the body that depends on it, and
to which it gives life. Therefore, if we wish to go to heaven in the
spiritual sense, we need not strain our spirit up or down, nor to one
side or the other.

* 'Through our bodies . . . in heaven': Philippians 3:20.

CHAPTER 61

That all physical matters are subject to spiritual matters.
This ruling is in accordance with the course of nature.

Nevertheless, it is necessary to lift up our eyes and our hands physically, as if to that physical heaven up there, in which the elements are moored. I am only referring to occasions when we are stirred to do this by the work of our spirit – otherwise we should not do this, because everything physical is subject to something spiritual, and is ruled in accordance, not in tension with it.

We have an example of this in the ascension of our Lord. When the ordained time arrived and he (who was never, nor ever could be, absent in his divinity) wanted to ascend physically in his humanity to his Father, because of the power of God the spirit, the humanity in physical form followed in unity of Person. It was most appropriate and fitting that the visible manifestation of this should be upwards.

This same subjection of the body to the spirit may be fully understood in the experience of contemplation by those who work at it. Whenever a soul consciously dedicates itself to this work, then, although the contemplative is himself unaware of the fact, the body, that perhaps before he began was leaning downwards, on one side or the other, for the sake of physical comfort, is immediately set upright by virtue of the spirit, following and imitating its spiritual work in a physical manner. It is most appropriate that this should be the case.

It is because of this appropriateness that a man, who is the most fitting corporeal being that God ever made, has not been created so as to stoop towards the earth, as do all other beasts, but stands upright, towards heaven, so that he should figure forth in his physical appearance the spiritual work of the soul, which is spiritually upright and not crooked. Pay attention to the fact that I say 'upright' in a spiritual and not physical sense. For how should a soul, which of its nature has no physical attributes at all, be strained upright physically? No, this cannot be.

Therefore, take care that you do not understand in the physical sense what is meant in the spiritual sense, even though it may be spoken of in physical terms, such as these: 'up', or 'down', 'in' or 'out', 'behind' or 'before', 'on one side' or 'on another'. For no matter how spiritual something is in itself, since speech is a physical activity performed with the tongue, which is an instrument of the body, it must always be spoken about in physical terms if it has to be discussed at all. But so what? Should it therefore be comprehended in the physical sense? No: only spiritually.

CHAPTER 62

How the contemplative may know when his spiritual work is
beneath or beyond him, and when it is together with him or
within him, and when it is above him and beneath God.

In order that you may better understand the spiritual sense of these
physical terms, I have it in mind to lay out to you the spiritual
signification of some terms that pertain to spiritual work, so that
you may infallibly discern when your spiritual work is beneath you
and beyond you, and when it is within you and equal to you, and
when it is above you and beneath God.

Every kind of physical thing is beyond your soul and naturally
beneath it. Indeed, even though the sun, the moon and all the stars
are literally above your body, they are still 'beneath' your soul.
Although all angels and souls are formed and adorned with grace and
virtues, through which they are above you in purity, nevertheless
they are still only equal with you in nature.

Within yourself, according to nature, are the powers of your
soul. The understanding, the reason and the will are its three
principal parts, and imagination and sensuality are its secondary
elements.

There is nothing above yourself, in nature, except God alone.

Wherever you find 'yourself' written about in relation to
spirituality, your soul should always be understood, and not your
body. The quality of your spiritual work shall be judged in
accordance with whatever the powers of your soul are working
on, and whether this is beneath, within or above you.

CHAPTER 63

The powers of the soul in general. How the understanding
in particular is a principal power, containing
all the other powers and their objects.

The understanding is a power which, to put it accurately, does not
work by itself. Reason and will, however, are two active faculties,
and so too are imagination and sensuality. The understanding
contains in itself all of these four powers and their activities. The
understanding is not said to work in any way, unless the act of
comprehension is treated as a form of work.

I do not call some of the powers of the soul primary and some
secondary because the soul is divisible, for that is not the case, but
because all their objects can be divided up. Some, such as spiritual
things, are primary, and others, such as all physical things, are
secondary. The two principal active faculties, reason and will,
work purely by themselves in all spiritual matters, without the help
of the other two secondary powers. Imagination and sensuality
operate more carnally on all physical materials, and co-operate
with the physical senses, whether reason and will are present or
absent. If they operated on their own, without the help of reason
and will, a soul would never acquire knowledge of the virtues and
other aspects of physical creatures, nor discover the causes of their
existence and the process of their creation.

Reason and will are thus called principal powers because they
work in pure spirit, without any kind of physicality; and imagination
and sensuality are secondary, because they work in the body with
their physical instruments, which are our five senses. The understanding is called a principal power because it spiritually contains in
itself not only all the other powers, but also all their objects. An
example follows.

CHAPTER 64

The other two principal powers, reason and will.
Their work before and after the Fall.

Reason is a power by which we divide evil from good, evil from what is worse and the good from what is better, the worse from the worst, the better from the best. Before man sinned, reason could have done all this naturally. Now, however, it is so blinded with original sin that it does not know how to perform this activity unless it is illuminated by grace. Both reason itself and its object are contained in the understanding.

Will is a power through which we choose good, after this has been determined by reason, and through which we love God, desire God and ultimately content ourselves with a thorough delight in and consent to God. Before man sinned, the will could not be deceived in its choice, in its loving, or in any of its activities, because it had the natural ability to savour each thing as it was. Now it may not do this unless it is anointed with grace. Because of infection from original sin, something which is only apparently good often tastes good to it. The understanding contains both the will and its object.

CHAPTER 65

The first secondary power, or imagination. Its activities and
its obedience to the will before and after the Fall.

Imagination is a power through which we represent to ourselves all
images of absent and present things. Both this and its objects are
contained in the understanding. Before man sinned, imagination
was so obedient to reason – to which it is a kind of servant – that it
never ministered to it the disorderly image of a physical creature,
or a delusion concerning a spiritual creature. Now it is not like this.
Only if it is restrained by the light of grace in the reason will it
cease, whether sleeping or waking, to represent different, disorderly images of physical creatures, or else some delusion, which is
nothing other than a physical conception of a spiritual thing, or else
a spiritual conception of a physical thing, and this is always make-
believe, and closely related to error.

  Such disobedience of the imagination may be clearly observed
when novices, who have recently withdrawn from the world
towards devotion, are at prayer. Before their imagination is largely
restrained by the light of grace in the reason – as it is by continual
meditation on spiritual things, such as their wretchedness, the
Passion and the kindness of our Lord God, and many other things
– they are unable to abandon the remarkable and diverse thoughts,
fantasies and images, which are ministered to and imprinted on
their minds by the light of the imagination's ingenuity. All this
disobedience is the painful consequence of original sin.

CHAPTER 66

The other secondary power, known as sensuality. Its activities
and its obedience to the will before and after sin

Sensuality is a power of the soul, ruling over and looking after
the physical senses through which we receive knowledge and
sensations concerning all physical creatures, whether they are
attractive or displeasing to us. It has two parts: one by which it
looks after our body's needs, and another by which it serves the
pleasures of the senses. This is the same power that complains when
the body lacks what is necessary, and that, in tending that need,
induces us to take more than is necessary when feeding and
satisfying our desires. It complains when it lacks material things
that please it, and is heartily delighted when they are present. It
complains when confronted by material things that it dislikes, and
is heartily delighted in their absence. Both this power and its object
are contained in the understanding.

Before man sinned, sensuality was so obedient to the will – in
relation to which it is like a servant – that it never ministered to it
any disorderly attachment or complaint about anything material
object, or any false spiritual attachment or irritation wrought in the
senses by a spiritual enemy. Now this is not the case, unless it is ruled
by grace in the will to endure the torment of original sin humbly and
tactfully. It experiences this pain in the absence of necessary pleasant
things and the presence of profitable, unpleasant things, and also has
to restrain itself from delight in the presence of necessary pleasant
things and from pleasure in the absence of profitable, unpleasant
things. Otherwise, it will wallow so wretchedly and intemperately
in the riches of this world and the delights of the foul flesh, like a pig
in the mire, that our whole life will be bestial and carnal, rather than
truly human or spiritual.

CHAPTER 67

*Anyone who is ignorant of the powers of a soul and their
ways of working may easily misunderstand spiritual
terms and spiritual work. How a soul is
made a 'god' through grace.*

Look, my spiritual friend, into what wretchedness we have fallen
because of sin! Why should we be surprised, therefore, if we are
blindly and easily deceived in the understanding of spiritual terms
and spiritual work? This is particularly the case with those who do
not yet know about the powers of their souls and the ways in
which they work. Whenever the mind is occupied with any
physical object, no matter how good the end is for which it
occupies our attention, nevertheless you are beneath yourself in
this activity, and beyond your soul. Whenever you feel your mind
preoccupied with the subtle states of the powers of your soul, and
their working on spiritual objects, such as your vices or virtues or
those of any creature that is spiritual and equal to you in nature, in
order that you might thereby acquire self-knowledge and increase
of perfection, then you are within yourself and equal to yourself.
However, whenever you feel your mind occupied with nothing
physical or spiritual, but only with the essence of God himself, as
may be proved by experience of contemplation, then you are
above yourself and beneath God.

You are 'above' yourself because, although you may not arrive at
it through nature, you attain that position by grace; that is to say,
you are united to God in spirit, love and concurrence of the will.
You are beneath God, because although in a way it could be said
that, during this time, God and you are not two but one in spirit —
to the extent that you or anyone else who experiences the perfection of contemplation may truly be called a 'god' on account of
such unity, as Scripture shows us — nevertheless, you are still
beneath him. This is because he is God by nature, without
beginning. You were at one time nothing in substance, and
afterwards, when turned into 'something' by his love and power,

made yourself worse than nothing through wilful sin. Only by his mercy, and not through your deserving it, may you be made a 'god' in grace, indivisibly united with him in spirit, both here and in the bliss of heaven eternally. So, although you are completely one with him in grace, you are still very far beneath him in nature.

Look, dear friend! You can partially appreciate from this that whoever does not know about the powers of their own soul, and about the ways in which they work, may very easily be deceived in understanding words that are written with a spiritual meaning. By this you may appreciate part of the reason why I did not dare directly invite you to show your desire to God, but coyly urged you to do your best to conceal it. I do this for fear lest you should interpret physically something that is intended in the spiritual sense.

CHAPTER 68

That 'nowhere' in physical terms is 'everywhere'
in spiritual terms. How our outer man calls
the work of this book 'nothing'.

When another man wishes to ask you to gather your powers
and your faculties together, and to worship God within, he is
speaking very properly, indeed, and no man more truly, in fact.
Nevertheless, for fear of misconceptions and the literal interpretation of such words, I would prefer not to ask you to do this. I
will ask one thing of you, though: take care that you are not
'within' yourself. Also, I do not want you to be 'outside' yourself,
nor yet above, nor behind, nor on one side nor on the other.

'Where, then,' you say, 'must I be? Nowhere, according to you!'
Now you have spoken well; for *that* is where I want you. This is
because 'nowhere' physically is 'everywhere' spiritually. Take
great care that your spiritual work happens 'nowhere' in the
physical sense; and then, your spirit will be wherever the object is
on which you voluntarily work in your mind, just as surely as your
body is in the place where you are physically. Even though all your
physical faculties cannot find anything on which to nourish themselves, because it seems to them that you are not doing anything,
then keep on at this 'nothing', and do it for the love of God. Don't
give up, therefore, but work hard in that 'nothing' with a vigilant
desire for God, whom no one may know. I assure you that I would
rather be 'nowhere' physically, wrestling with that imageless
'nothing', than to be so great a lord that I could be everywhere
physically whenever I wanted, cheerfully toying with all of this
'anything' as a lord does with his possessions.

Abandon this 'everywhere' and this 'anything' in favour of this
'nowhere' and this 'nothing'. Do not care if your faculties cannot
make sense of this 'nothing', for surely I love it the better for that.
It is so worthy a thing in itself that they cannot make sense of it.
This nothing may be better felt than seen, for it is purely imageless

and very dark to those who have looked at it only for a little while. Nevertheless, to speak more accurately, a soul is 'blinded' in experiencing it more because of the abundance of spiritual light than on account of any lack of physical light. Who calls it nothing? Our outer man, surely, and not our inner self. Our inner man calls it All, because he has properly learned from it to make sense of all things, physical or spiritual, without any particular attachment to any one thing by itself.

CHAPTER 69

How a man's disposition is wondrously changed through
the spiritual apprehension of this 'nothing',
when it is performed 'nowhere'.

A man's affection is remarkably transformed in the spiritual apprehension of this 'nothing' when it is carried out 'nowhere'. For on
the first occasion that a person looks at it, he finds depicted on it all
the particular sins that he committed since he was born, whether
physical or spiritual, confidentially or obscurely. However he turns
it about, they will always appear before his eyes, until, with much
hard work, many deep sighs and many bitter floods of tears, he has
largely rubbed them away.

Sometimes in this process he thinks that to look at it is like
looking upon hell, because it seems to him that he despairs of
winning through from that torment to the perfection of spiritual
rest. Many come thus far inwards, but, because of the degree of
torment that they feel, and because of the lack of comfort, they go
back towards attachment to physical things, seeking carnal pleasures
outside themselves, because of the spiritual comforts that they have
not earned, and which they would have enjoyed if they had stayed.

Anyone who stays feels some comfort, and has some hope of
perfection, for he feels and sees that many of his particular old sins
are largely rubbed away by the help of grace. He still feels pain
together with this, but he realises that it will cease, because it is
diminishing. He does not call it 'hell', therefore, but 'purgatory'.
Sometimes he cannot find a particular sin written on it, but thinks of
it as a kind of lump, he does not know what, but nothing other than
himself; and then it may be called the stump and the pain of original
sin. Sometimes he thinks that it is paradise or heaven, on account of
the diverse wonderful delights and comforts, joys and blessed virtues
that he finds there. On other occasions, he thinks that it is God,
because of the peace and tranquillity that he finds there.

Yes, let him think whatever he likes, for he shall always find a
cloud of unknowing between him and God.

CHAPTER 70

Just as we begin most readily to arrive at knowledge of
spiritual things when our physical faculties begin to
fail, so by the failing of our spiritual powers, we
most readily begin to arrive at the knowledge
of God, as far as is possible through
grace in this life.

Therefore, work hard at this 'nothing' and this 'nowhere', and abandon your outward physical senses and all that they work on, for I assure you that this work may not be comprehended by them. You cannot make out anything with your eyes unless by its length, breadth, smallness and greatness, and whether it is round, square, far or near. Likewise, you may not discern anything with your ears unless it is a noise or some kind of sound; nor with your nose, unless it is a stench or a sweet smell; or by your tastebuds, unless it is sour or sweet, salt or fresh, bitter or pleasant; or by your sense of touch, unless it is hot or cold, hard or tender, soft or sharp. Neither God nor spiritual things have any of these qualities or quantities. Therefore, abandon your outward senses, and do not employ them either within or without. All those who dedicate themselves to inner contemplation, and think that they should either hear, smell or see, taste or feel spiritual things, either inside or outside themselves, are certainly deceived and are working incorrectly and unnaturally. The senses have been naturally ordained so that through them men should achieve knowledge of all outward physical things, and should not achieve knowledge of spiritual things through their activities.

We may achieve this, though, by their failings, as in this example: when we read or hear some particular things being discussed, and realise that our outward senses cannot tell us anything about them, then we may be certain that those are spiritual and not physical matters.

It is the same with our spiritual senses, when we work at the knowing of God himself. For no matter how much spiritual understanding a man has, knowing all created spiritual things, the understanding can never bring him to the knowledge of an uncreated spiritual thing, which is God. A measure of success may be retrieved from this kind of failure, though, because what it fails to know is nothing but God himself. This is why Saint Dionysius said 'The most spiritual knowledge of God is that which is acquired by unknowing.'*

Certainly, anyone who reads Saint Dionysius' books will find that his words clearly affirm all that I say from the beginning of this treatise to the end. At this stage, I would prefer not to cite him or any other doctor in favour of my arguments more explicitly. There was a time when men thought it an aspect of humility to say nothing original unless they confirmed it with reference to Scripture and the words of the doctors; and now this practice has degenerated into mere ingenuity and the parade of learning. You have no need of it, and therefore I do not use this method. Whoever has ears, let him hear; and whoever is stirred to believe, let him believe, for otherwise he will not.

* 'Saint Dionysius said . . . ': in *The Divine Names* (*De Divinis Nominibus*), chapter 7:3: 'He is known through knowledge and through unknowing . . . He is known to all from all things and he is known to no one from anything . . . the most divine knowledge of God, that which comes through unknowing, is achieved in a union far beyond mind, when mind turns away from all things, even from itself . . . ' (see the translation referred to under 'Further Reading', pp. xx–xxi).

CHAPTER 71

*Some may not experience the perfection of contemplation
except in a state of rapture, and some may
experience it ordinarily, and at will.*

Some think this matter so difficult and formidable that they say it
may not be achieved without much hard work in advance, nor
understood except fitfully, and even then in a state of ecstasy. To
these men I will answer to the best of my feeble ability and say that
it is all done at God's disposal, in accordance with the spiritual
ability of those to whom the grace of contemplation and spiritual
work are given.

There are some that may not achieve it without much prolonged
spiritual exercise; and still they only feel the perfection of contemplation fitfully, and in that special summons from our Lord which
is called rapture. There are some who are so subtle in grace and
spirit, and so intimate with God in this grace of contemplation, that
they may have it when they wish, under normal conditions, as
when sitting, moving, standing, or kneeling. During this time they
are in full possession of all their faculties, whether physical or
spiritual, and may use them if they wish, not without some
hindrance, but without any great impediment. Moses is a type of
the first kind of contemplative, and Aaron, the priest of the temple,
represents the second kind.

This is because the grace of contemplation is represented by the
ark of the Covenant* in the Old Testament, and contemplatives are
represented by those who were most closely involved with this ark,
as the story will show. This work and this grace are most fittingly
likened to that ark, because, just as the ark contained all the jewels
and the relics of the temple, so this little impulse of love contains all
the virtues of a man's soul, which is the spiritual temple of God.

---

* 'ark of the Covenant'. The full account is given in Exodus 25–40. Richard
of Saint Victor relates this episode to the contemplative life in *Benjamin Major*.

Before he could come to see this ark, and know how it should be constructed, Moses had some hard work to do: he climbed up to the top of the mountain, and remained there, spending six days in a cloud, waiting for the seventh day, on which our Lord condescended to show him the way in which the ark was to be constructed. Moses' long work and the tardiness of his epiphany may be taken to signify those who may not achieve the perfection in contemplation without a long period of work beforehand, and even then only sporadically and when God's will permits it.

However, what Moses could not see except on occasion, and then not without a great deal of hard work, Aaron could observe in the temple behind the veil as often as he wished to enter, because of his particular duties there. Aaron may be taken to signify all those about whom I spoke above, who, by their spiritual skills, with the help of grace, may experience contemplative perfection as often as they like.

CHAPTER 72

*A contemplative should not judge or think about another
in the light of his own experience.*

Look! By this example you may see that the one who cannot experience the perfection of this work except with a great deal of work, and then only occasionally, may easily be deceived if he speaks about, thinks about and judges other men according to his own experience, saying that they cannot achieve it except occasionally, and then not without hard work. In the same manner, he that may have it at will may likewise be deceived if he judges all others along the same lines, saying that they may have it when they wish. Abandon this attitude: surely one cannot think like this, because perhaps, when it pleases God, whose who may not on the first occasion experience it except fitfully, and then not without hard work, may afterwards have it when they wish, as often as they like. We have an example of this in Moses. At first he could only see the ark occasionally, and not without hard work on the mountain, but afterwards he saw it as often as he wished, in the valley.

CHAPTER 73

The three benefits of contemplation are represented in the
figures of Moses, Bezaleel and Aaron, in their concern
for the ark of the Covenant, for the grace of
contemplation is signified by the ark.

There were three men who were chiefly involved with the Ark of
the Old Testament: Moses, Bezaleel and Aaron. Moses learned from
our Lord on the mountain how it should be made; Bezaleel created
it and made it in the valley, in accordance with the instructions
issued on the mountain; and Aaron kept it as part of his guardianship
of the temple, and could see and touch it as often as he wished.

The three ways in which we profit by the grace of contemplation
are represented by these three types. Sometimes we profit only by
grace, and then we are like Moses, who, for all the climbing and the
work that he did on the mountain, could not see it except occasionally, and then that sight was only granted by our Lord when he
wished, and not because Moses had earned that right. Sometimes
we profit in this grace by our own spiritual skills, helped with grace,
and then we are like Bezaleel, who could not seek the Ark before
he had made it by his own hands, helped by the instructions given
to Moses on the mountain. Sometimes we profit in this grace
through other men's teaching, in which case we are like Aaron,
who had in his keeping and could habitually see and feel, when it
pleased him, the ark that Bezaleel had created with his hands.

Look, dear friend: although I am expressing myself in a jejune and
ignorant way, although I am a wretch and unworthy to teach
anyone, I am performing the duty of Bezaleel, making and bringing
this spiritual ark to your hands, as it were, in my work. You must
work, though, and far better and more worthily than I do, if you
wish to be Aaron; that is to say, keep working on my behalf and
yours. Do this, I beg you, for the love of God Almighty. And since
we have both been called by God to work at contemplation, I beg
you for the love of God to fulfil on your part what is lacking on
mine.

CHAPTER 74

How contemplation is never read, heard or discussed by
a sympathetic soul, without it experiencing a feeling
of true accord with its effects. A repetition of
the warnings issued in the prologue.

If you think that this kind of work is not suitable for your physical and spiritual disposition, you may safely abandon it and, with good spiritual advice, take up another without incurring any blame. Then I would beg you to excuse me, because I truly wanted you to benefit from my simple knowledge in this writing. That was my intention. Therefore, read it over twice or three times, and the more often the better; you will understand it all the more, to the extent, perhaps, that some passage that seemed very difficult to you at the first or second reading will later seem very easy to you.

It seems impossible, to my way of thinking, that anyone who is inclined to contemplation should read it, or speak about it, or else hear it being read or spoken about, without that same person feeling a true concurrence with the effect of this work. If you think it does you good, thank God sincerely, and pray for me for the love of God.

Proceed, then. I beg you for the love of God that you do not let anyone else see this book, unless you think him suitable, given what I have written beforehand in this book concerning types of men and when they should engage in contemplation. If you let any such men see it, then I beg you to urge them to take their time to read it all. For perhaps there may be something in it, at the beginning, or in the middle, which is incomplete and not immediately explained in full. But if the explanation is not given immediately, it is dealt with soon after, or else at the end. Thus, if a man saw one part and not the other, he should perhaps be easily misled. Therefore, I beg you to do as I say. If you think that there is any material in it that you wish to have dilated further than it is here, let me know which it is and what you think of it, and, from my simple knowledge, I will improve upon it if I can.

Crude jokers, gossips and carpers, idiots, morons and people who go in for all kinds of sniping must never read this book. I never intended to address any of it to them. Therefore I would prefer that neither they nor speculative types, whether learned or ignorant, should hear it – yes, even though they may be very good at the active life – because it is not suitable for them.

CHAPTER 75

Certain signs whereby a someone may prove whether or not
he has been called by God to the work of contemplation.

All those who read this book, or hear it being read or discussed, and
think that it is a good and pleasant thing, are not necessarily called
by God to work at contemplation on account of the pleasant
stirring that they experience while it is being read. Such a stirring
may perhaps come more from the mind's natural curiosity than
from any calling of grace.

If they wish to test the source of this stirring, they must do so in
the following manner. First, they must look to see if they have
previously done their best to enable themselves to be cleansed in
their consciences, according to the judgement of Holy Church and
with the agreement of their spiritual adviser. If this is the case, then
so far so good. If they wish to understand this further, though, they
must look to see if it is always coming into their mind more
regularly than any other kind of spiritual exercise. If they think that
anything they do, whether physical or spiritual, is only performed
to the satisfaction of their conscience if this intimate impulse of
love is the most important aspect of their spiritual work, then it is
a sign that they have been called by God to this work; otherwise,
they have not.

I am not saying that it shall last forever and dwell continually in the
minds of all those who have been called to work at contemplation.
That is certainly not the case. The actual perception of it is often
withdrawn from a young spiritual apprentice for various reasons.
Sometimes it happens so that he may not become too intimate with
it, and think that it is largely in his own power, to experience as and
when he likes. Such a belief would be pride. Pride is always the
reason why that feeling of grace is withdrawn. This may not always
be actual pride but potential pride, which would flourish if this
feeling of grace had not been withdrawn. Thus some young fools
often think that God is their enemy, when he is their good friend.
Sometimes it is withdrawn because of their carelessness; and when

this happens, they immediately afterwards feel a bitter pain that torments them very harshly. Sometimes our Lord will delay it with a strategem, because he wants, by means of such a delay, to make it grow and be treasured more, as when something which has been lost for a long time is discovered afresh and experienced all over again. This is the most important and one of the most direct signs by which someone may know whether or not he is called to work at this activity. After a delay and a long break in contemplation, he feels that when it comes suddenly (as it does, and not through any indirect means) he then has a greater fervour of desire and a greater yearning to work at contemplation than he ever had before, to the extent that often I think that the joy he has in finding it is greater than any sorrow he experienced through losing it. If this is what happens, it is certainly a true sign, without any mistake, that he has been called by God to work at contemplation, whatever he is or has been.

For it is not what you are, not what you have been, that God looks at with his merciful eyes, but what you would be. Saint Gregory affirms* that 'all holy desires grow through delays; and if they wane by delays, then they were never holy desires.' For when someone feels less and less joy in discovering new things and suddenly being presented with his old desires, however natural and good they may be, they are not holy desires. Saint Augustine speaks* about this desire when he says that 'the whole of a Christian man's life is nothing other than holy desire.'

Farewell, dear friend, with God's blessing and mine! I beseech Almighty God that you and all those on earth who love God may have true peace, wise counsel, spiritual comfort and abundance of grace for evermore. Amen.

* 'Saint Gregory affirms . . . ': in his *Homiliarum in Evangelia* ii, 25. 'Saint Augustine speaks . . . ': in *In Epistolam Ioannis ad Parthos*, IV, ii, 6.